To Be
Mayor
of Vancouver

by
James Green

Order this book online at www.trafford.com
or email orders@trafford.com

Most Trafford titles are also available at major online book retailers.

Note for Librarians: A cataloguing record for this book is available from Library
and Archives Canada at www.collectionscanada.ca/amicus/index-e.html

Print information available on the last page.

ISBN: 978-1-4251-2700-8 (sc)

Trafford rev. 01/19/2018

 www.trafford.com

North America & international
toll-free: 1 888 232 4444 (USA & Canada)
fax: 812 355 4082

DEDICATION

This book is dedicated to my family; Marlies, Arlana and Erin who are my strength.

I dedicate this book to my brothers Gary and Truman, my sister Gertrude and to the memory of my sister Jackie.

I also dedicate this book to my mother, Annie.

TRIBUTE

The other candidates who ran for Mayor of Vancouver as independents in 2005 deserve a tribute here as they had the determination to step up to the plate.

ACKNOWLEDGEMENTS

This book would not have happened without the support and hard work of Marlies, my dear wife. I also thank my daughter Arlana who saved the campaign with her guidance, hard work and support. Furthermore, I thank my daughter Erin for being my literary inspiration. It does not matter what I decide to do in life, I always have the support of these three, who are my life and whom I love more than air. I thank my friends Ed Rychkun, Rand Chatterjee, Hope Rychkun, Tracey Gabert, and Jonathan Moran for their ongoing support and assistance with this project.

CAST OF CHARACTERS

James Green   Me, the author of this book and an independent candidate for Mayor in the 2005 election.

Sam Sullivan   Current Mayor and member of the NPA. Previously a four-term councillor.

NPA   NPA - Non Partisan Association. Sam Sullivan's party.

Jim Green   Vancouver City Councillor from 2002 to 2005 and the Vision Vancouver candidate for Mayor in the 2005 election.

Larry Campbell   Mayor of Vancouver during the election and a member of Vision Vancouver, the party Jim Green and Larry Campbell formed. Currently a Canadian Senator.

Vision Vancouver Current opposition to NPA, formerly members of COPE.

COPE The 2002-2005 Vancouver City Council that included Jim Green as a councillor and Larry Campbell as Mayor. Councillor David Cadman is the only remaining vestige of their former glory.

FOREW0RD

It is Christmas Eve 2006 and I am watching the DVD *World Trade Centre*. The catastrophe and the loss of life of this act of terror is very sad and painful. For some reason, the movie spurred me on to finally finish this book, as all stories should be told. Up to this time I believed that the story was too negative and could be harmful to me should I decide to run for Mayor in 2008. Given the recent incredible statements being made by the other Green and others in the Vision Vancouver Camp, I now feel I have no choice. I feel that Vancouver citizens deserve to know the truth and what really happened during the campaign. Following is my account of my campaign to become the Mayor of Vancouver, BC in 2005.

The response to my entry into the Mayor's race was both shocking and exciting. The number of votes I received were surprising to some and disappointing to me. The controversy surrounding my campaign was phenomenal and has not dissipated.

There has been much intrigue and interest as well as misinformation as to what happened and who was doing what to whom regarding the 2005 Vancouver civic election campaign to become Mayor of Vancouver. Speculation about how I received 4273 votes to come in third out of twenty (more votes than any other independent has received in recent history) has been a-plenty. Many have asked what role my candidacy played in the defeat of Jim Green and in the election of Sam Sullivan as the Mayor of Vancouver. There have been many charges of illegal and questionable behaviour on my part. Some suggested Jim Green took votes away from me. Others asked why I ran in the first place and why I didn't run for council, parks board or school board first. Vision Vancouver, one of the two major parties in Vancouver, went as far as calling for an inquiry into what they were calling the James Green Affair. The media, who somewhat ignored my campaign, made me a media spectacle after the campaign. At the time this alarmed me and now I clearly understand why. The media, and their role in the elections, will be explained here. Still, some say I had no experience and had a lot of nerve running for Mayor in the first place.

Many good people supported and helped me, sent me e-mails, made phone calls wishing me good luck, and complimented me on a job well done. Some have been inspired by me and others have called me filth, an imposter and a sleaze. One guy, on line, said I should be dragged out into the street and shot.

Some very questionable people will be revealed here. Many insinuated that the NPA paid me to run for Mayor to stop Jim Green. On the streets of this city many people have an opinion about me and my campaign for Mayor. Most people I meet are supportive and positive. I have enjoyed the comments and questions I still receive when I travel throughout the Lower Mainland.

My immediate family and friends have shown me a great deal of love and support and have shown how wonderful people can be. Larry Campbell, the COPE/NDP/Vision-supported former Mayor of Vancouver turned Liberal Senator, has called me a criminal and has refused to be in the same room as me. Jim Green and members of his Vision Vancouver Party have called me every name imaginable during and after the election.

Nevertheless, after the election I have been covered by all major and not so major radio, magazine, newspaper and television reporters.

The funniest comment about me was by columnist Steve Burgess who referred to me as the Human Homonym. Thousands still wonder what really happened with my campaign. Was there a conspiracy and who is James Green? Like me, many question if one ill-intentioned telephone call made by Sam Sullivan really constitutes or proves there was a conspiracy and election fraud.

I am sure Vision Vancouver and their backroom boys and girls still question whether their strategy, of ignoring me publicly and smearing me behind my back, was the right way to go. Jim Green, the other Green running for Mayor, even in 2007 holds to the story that my name was the reason he lost the election and that he and Vision took the highest road they possibly could in the campaign. We shall see.

As of November 2006, Jim Green stated on a television program that the NPA put me up to running. He has continued to insinuate that the NPA had bankrolled my campaign. However groundless these charges are, he keeps making them. Jim also has stated time and time again that there will shortly be more released about the relationship between James Green, Sam Sullivan and the NPA.

This book will reveal the character assassinations, the libel, defamation, slander and dirty tricks that were directed at me and some of my supporters during the campaign. This book will tell the story of who supported me financially.

1. Did I campaign aggressively or was my campaign invisible?
2. Did I have any chance of winning the race to be Mayor?
3. Did I run to confuse voters?
4. Did I have a vision or a platform?
5. How did I get my campaign office and that great bus?

This book leaves nothing out and tells all, from my early years, to my daughters' support, to the big black bus, to my perhaps bogus campaign manager, to all of the wonderful times I had meeting thousands of people on the campaign trail.

This story is hard hitting and will whet the appetites of readers who love scandals, human interest stories, or those who just enjoy a story of one against the odds. Political junkies will love this story.

Lastly, this book will set the record straight and reveal many truths about politicians and politics in Vancouver.

CHAPTER ONE

Election Night November 19, 2005

Election night began when my forty foot campaign bus arrived at my home at 8 pm and collected me, my daughter-turned-campaign manager Arlana, my wife Marlies, my videographer Jonathan Moran and a family friend Leanne Gillespie. I was relaxed and low key and still felt I had a good chance. I was happy as we had done a good job and reached thousands of voters. I had no idea of what was about to happen once the votes were counted and the news was out. The firestorm I would be hit with would throw me for a loop for some time.

My campaign bus, the focus of a great deal of controversy and now known as the James Green Bus, traveled to the Elderado Hotel on Kingsway in Vancouver. Jamie Lee Hamilton, a rather flamboyant candidate for council, had invited all independent candidates to a party to watch the results come in on a big screen TV, have a few drinks and celebrate our campaigns.

When we arrived at the hotel room, we were greeted by a friendly group and were told to "pull up a bed and watch the results come in". I had a glass of wine and made a few jokes. Some results came in and my numbers looked grim. I had three hundred or so votes and Jim and Sam had pulled ahead. I was, of course, disappointed.

At this point a Vancouver Courier reporter named Cheryl Rossi, a very polite young woman, asked me to do the interview she had confirmed with me a few days before. We went to the lobby of the hotel. She grilled me for almost 40 minutes about much that will be covered in this book. This long interview resulted in these few lines actually published in the Courier newspaper.

> "8:55 pm   Independent   Mayoral candidate James Green, dapper in a black pinstriped suit, appeared at the gathering. He, his wife, daughter and another young woman were eager to see the results because they couldn't find an election broadcast on Green's 40-foot-long   electioneering   bus' satellite TV. Green had refused the Courier access to the bus earlier in the evening."

The interview, which had caused me to miss most of the returns, ended and I went back to the room to say goodbye. I did not pay any attention to the numbers on the screen. We boarded the bus and drove people home. All was calm and friendly, but I was very pensive and quiet. Everyone on board respected my space, and we did not discuss the election. We all said goodbye to John, our driver. John had been our driver for 10 days and he was always helpful, supportive, friendly and totally cooperative. We would miss John with his smile and sense of humor. We left the bus and climbed the steps leading to our front door. It was a quiet night. No one was on the street and the silence was a little eerie. My daughter went in first, next my wife Marlies and lastly me. Before I hit the top of the stairs, Arlana shouted to us that a reporter on television was defending me and some guy was insulting me. Before I had a chance to take my coat off or go to the television, the telephone rang. It was a reporter named Myk Smith from CKNW Radio who was pumped up, excited and fired off a volley of silly and somewhat ridiculous questions. I remember Christy Clark was in the studio with him. I did not understand why people were talking about me and why this guy was calling me until he asked how I felt about getting 4273 votes. He said I caused Jim Green's defeat and asked who put me up to it, and was the NPA behind my campaign.

I gave very terse answers to his uninformed speak and ended the call. I went to watch television and the finals were in. Sam Sullivan NPA 61,543 - Jim Green Vision Vancouver 57,796 - James Green 4273 votes. I was resigned to coming in third and did not anticipate what would happen next.

That night, and for the next 10 days, my world became a media circus and the city became a hotbed of speculation and polarization, pro and anti James Green. I would have loved to have had all of this attention during the campaign, but must admit I enjoyed all of the time spent setting the record straight. I knew I had done nothing wrong and I answered all questions candidly. Arlana accompanied me to all of the interviews and she helped me stay focused. All media called for an interview, and I dove into this abyss of speculation, supposition, confrontation, assumed scandal and intrigue. My daughter Arlana, as well as running much of my campaign, now became my communications manager. The emails and the telephone calls did not stop. Not having a campaign office, the Starbucks at Cambie Street and 19th became my outdoor studio. I gave numerous TV interviews and at three in the morning election night I was finally in bed when the phone rang. The caller asked my name and when I said "James Green" he said "f... you" and made a veiled threat as he hung up. Somewhat dazed, I hung up and fell asleep. I do not scare easily, though I did call the police the next day. They were very good at reassuring me and told me if I had more calls or any other problems to feel free to call and they would be at my house as soon as possible. I was thankful to the Vancouver Police Department for this.

The Day After The Night Before
The questions and interviews are too many to recount here. The inaccurate stories on television, radio and in newspapers shocked me, but educated me as well.

Walking down the street the next day, November 20, it was odd as so many people had no problem telling me what they felt. In most cases people were positive. Many said they voted for me. One guy did drive by in a van and expressed himself with his middle finger.

The limited coverage, that resulted from my 40 minute interview on election night, left me feeling very uncomfortable. The story would never be told and no one, not even the media, really wanted it to be. Seems "less said the better" was still the plan. At the time I had no idea of what would follow.

The emails were the most revealing and told me I had been wise to run for Mayor. Following is one of the most heart warming emails I received.

Emailed to me Monday November 21, 2005
Dear Mr. Green:

> Congratulations on coming in third in the Mayor's race. I hope you will continue in politics. I met you several years ago when you ran a music program at False Creek Elementary and you made a huge impact in my son's life. Andrew, who with your help sang a Beatles solo and helped MC the great musical you developed for them, went on to sing in a gospel choir and then studied acting at Capilano College and the Lyric Acting School. His career, started with your influence, was unfortunately cut short when he was murdered three years ago but I still want to thank you for making his short life

meaningful. I hope I will get a chance to vote for you in the future. You are an asset to Vancouver. Take care. Lana (Andrew's mom).

I remembered Lana's son, in my grade seven music class. He was a wonderfully talented and kind-hearted boy. I cried and wished I could have known her son as an adult.

And a not so friendly email.

Catherine Welsh, a woman I have never met, emailed me.
Wednesday, November 23, 2005
Demand for public inquiry

> As the days go by since the municipal election it becomes increasingly clear, that a great injustice is taking place and democracy itself no longer exists in Vancouver. With the admission of Mr. Sullivan that he was indeed in contact with Mr. James Green prior to the election and then lied about it, an inquiry needs to take place immediately. This is not the first

time Mr. Sullivan has been caught
on tape in an outright lie.

In other emails I was dubbed a sleaze, liar, spoiler
and sarcastically thanked for ruining Jim Green's
chance to be Mayor. There were also those, just
as uninformed, who seriously thanked me for the
same reason.

Both the supportive and hostile emails I now see
in a positive light, as people had been provoked
to express their opinions and I realize this is a
good thing. The attention assured me of one
thing. I could be Mayor next time.

CHAPTER TWO

Campaign Briefing or "Know the Sleaze Factor"

Before we get into it any further, let me recall a meeting I had with John Dormer, the former Mayor of Kamloops, BC. When I told John I was going to run, in July 2005, he said he would help me as much as he could. Well, he came to my campaign office for a very important meeting, perhaps the most significant meeting of the entire campaign.

We began with what I needed to become Mayor. Funny thing, and maybe an oversight on our part, we didn't discuss the name game as I had changed my name to James and that was that. The conversation led to the dirty tricks Jim Green and his Vision Team and Sam Sullivan and the NPA would play on me. It is interesting to note that most of John's warnings came true. I did not take what John said to heart, as I could not bring myself to believe that anyone could sink so low to win an election. I was wrong, very wrong. Here's the list of dirties:

1. They would email me a virus that would likely shut down my computer.

2. They would plant any negative information they could make up, or twist information and release it to the media who would have no problem printing it.

3. They would plant a mole in my campaign.

4. They would attempt to have a women get me in compromising situation and use it against me.

5. They would threaten or at least warn and intimidate anyone they could who might support me.

6. They would attempt to dry up or ward away any financial support I might gain.

7. They would attempt to exclude me from the campaign as much as possible.

8. Overall, they would discredit me in any way they could.

At this time I thought John's warnings were a little far-fetched and a little outrageous. I blocked them out and did not even begin to believe I needed a strategy to deal with something like this as I doubted it could happen. Overall my denial was perhaps my undoing.

A Smoking Gun?

The story that caused the firestorm and motivated Vision Vancouver to call for an inquiry into the election was filed by a CTV reporter named Rob Brown. Brown's faulty reporting fired up Jim Green, Larry Campbell, Vision Vancouver and gave them what they thought was the smoking gun. Brown's story, they were sure, proved that Sam Sullivan, the NPA and James Green were in cahoots. As the days passed, this story was unraveled and many people had egg on their faces. Some had crow for dinner. Many refused to accept the truth.

Brown's story, as he crafted it, seemed to prove that Sam had called the owners of the Azure Lounge and Grill on the Plaza of Nations to get me a campaign office. Brown interviewed, by telephone and while in camera, one of the owners of the restaurant, a Julius Simon, who told him in broken English, that Sam had called to see if Simon could help me acquire a campaign office in the Plaza of Nations.

The next day Vision Vancouver, Jim Green's party, in full gloat called for an inquiry into what they called the James Green Affair. Vision hoped the office story, though untrue, furnished them with enough evidence to prove that Sam had helped me get the office in the first place, that I was a fraud and imposter and that the election was tainted.

Before we go on please ask yourself: If you were on the NPA payroll, like Vision alleged that I was, would you do something as obvious as move into a complex where the NPA candidate for Mayor had an office as well? Would you call the Vancouver Sun to come to your office and take a picture of you at your office and publish it in the newspaper?

Sad thing for my detractors was the fact that I had set up my campaign office next to the Azure Lounge and Grill on the Plaza of Nations before Sam was even the NPA candidate. Sam and Christy Clark were still fighting to become the NPA candidate for Mayor when I moved into my office. The gun wasn't even loaded, let alone smoking.

To subtract more fuel from the CTV office story fire, I was evicted from the office in question with one day's notice and all Sam really did, he said, was to call the owner to see why I was kicked out. Sam said he called so he could use this against Jim Green. Sam said he had been forwarded an email I had sent out to a friend of mine that stated that I felt I had been bullied out by Jim Green. In fact, I believed it was a toss-up. It could have been Sam or Jim who got me evicted. There is not a doubt that there was political motivation behind the eviction. After the campaign the Courier newspaper reported that Daisen Gee-Wing, the manager of the complex, had donated money to the NPA and Sam's campaign and to Vision and Jim Green's campaign. In the Courier newspaper, Daisen said he had offered me the office back (news to me) and that the eviction was not political, even though the space remains empty to this day. I also learned that Sam had complained to Daisen about my being in the office. Daisen evicted me, so why would he offer me the office back, especially since he contributed money to both Sam's and Jim's campaigns.

Sam promised to give the mystery email to the media, but to this day he has not. I am interested in finding out who was sharing my emails with Sam Sullivan. Perhaps it was my campaign manager or Frank Palmer.

I need to know, how does one useless and ineffective telephone call represent or prove Sam Sullivan and the NPA financed my campaign or were in contact with me or helped me in any way?

Around this time, and before the late news, Mi-Jung Lee of CTV News phoned me to corroborate Rob's report, although it had already been aired earlier in the evening. I told her Rob had it wrong. I thought I had set the record straight. However, the 11:30 pm news was somewhat briefer and therefore more accurate, but still left doubt in many minds. They still had Sam getting me the office.

CTV's Rob Brown interviewed me a few weeks later at City Hall. Off camera Brown expressed how sorry he was that he had gotten the story wrong. The sorry fact here is that reporters like Brown are allowed to file untrue stories.

The Vancouver Sun jumped on board this train to nowhere, as did all media, and reported this under the headline: "Sam Sullivan Helped James Green". The reporter of this headline was Frances Bula.

Sam told his stories in his usual fool-the-media fashion, which was to tell varied versions of the same story and thus tie the media up in a reporting knot. What kills me is that Sam's approach and his "poor li'l 'ole me, nice guy" image works. He is nothing but a traditional politician with a strong team of spin doctors, handlers and strategists surrounding him.

Sam told me at the All Candidates Meeting at Shaw Cable, "They underestimate me and then I strike like a rattlesnake."

What made Sam seem dishonest, and cast a negative light on me, was his answer a few days before this office story broke. Reporters had asked him if he had any contact with James Green or did any of his people have any contact. Sam said he would be very upset if that were the case.

I actually think he may have forgotten the short talk we had at Shaw. In passing, in a hallway at Shaw Cable in North Vancouver, Sam said hi and that he had heard I had been kicked out of the office and did I want him to make a call to see if he could get it back. It was fine with me and I said so, all the time laughing to myself, thinking that Sam likely got me kicked out in the first place. There is no election fraud here, no benefit and just a man named Sam Sullivan making a dumb call to look like a good guy and to find some dirt on Jim Green. In fact, Sam may have feigned his belief that Jim Green got me kicked out. I had based my belief that Jim Green was the culprit on the fact that Jim's minion, Geoff Meggs, had asked me on October 17 at SFU Harbour Centre at an All Candidates Meeting, if I was out of my office yet. He had no way of knowing I had just been given the boot. At the time I assumed he and Green had something to do with it. It also came out later, after the election, that, previous to this whole debacle, Sam had made a call to the landlords to express his concern that I was in the office and that it might look bad for him. I must be clear here, whatever Sam did regarding the office, did not help me as I did not get it back and in fact, I moved home.

CHAPTER THREE

Who is James Green?

My goal here is to tell you the main aspects of my life so you will understand what makes me tick, how I arrived at the confidence level that I could be Mayor. From this short story I hope you can see that failing to meet a challenge is foreign to me.

I was born on September 8, 1947 in the Royal Columbia Hospital in New Westminster, BC. My mother has spoken for years about how difficult the birth was and that I almost didn't make it, but I fought back and survived. In fact she says it was incredible how strong I became and how I started beating the odds way back then. My father, who later died in the 70s, was named Carl Green. My mother Annie, who is still alive today, is 90 years old. Dad and Mom divorced shortly after I was born.

After the birth, I left the hospital and was transported to our home in Webster's Corners, Haney, BC. We lived in a two room shack. When I was three years old we moved to Newton in Surrey, to somewhat larger quarters. We were very poor.

The house we moved to was too small for the six of us, so we moved to another house that had four rooms but no indoor plumbing. It was at 6635 Roebuck Road in Newton. There was seldom enough food to go around. We did have five acres that served as a source of fun and survival.

In Newton we had some very caring neighbours who watched over us kids when we were left alone, and helped us. I happily remember a turkey mysteriously being found on our porch at Christmas.

We made extra money by cutting down and selling Christmas trees or by pulling the bark off Cascara trees and selling it to a company, who in turn sold it to a pharmaceutical company. I was a resourceful kid and worked in neighbour's gardens who paid me in vegetables or fruit. I also got my brothers and sisters jobs picking strawberries and beans on farms in Surrey. I was known as little Jimmy Green and mother says I was the sweetest and nicest child in the world. To bring home the food, clothe us, pay the bills and the mortgage, mother worked at my aunt's night club named the Dixie Chicken Inn on Seymour Street in Vancouver. This club was beside the

Penthouse in Vancouver. She was paid $2.00 per hour. On weekends I went to work with her and in the evenings I directed cars to parking spots on the small lot. I was paid twenty-five cents per car which allowed me to go shopping most Saturdays on Granville Street. I remember such places as Love's Skillet, The Peter Pan, The Crack-a-Joke. The Marine Building was the tallest Building in the city. The Dixie Chicken Inn was one of Vancouver's first cabarets and opened in 1935. Before working there, my mother worked in service as a maid in some of the wealthiest homes in Vancouver. She did whatever job she could to support her family of five children.

Between ages 6 to 10 I hung out with the wealthiest kids in Newton, who lived on Panorama Ridge. They treated me well and didn't seem to care if I was poor or black. I remember swimming in pools, eating dinners at well-presented tables and being driven home in fancy big cars. So be clear here, I grew up Canadian and proud. Black and poor was secondary and not an important part of who I was. mother, even though she was poor, always carried herself like royalty, very classy. She spoke well and was well read. I was so proud of her. She passed on her values of hard work, self pride, and courage to me. Imagine one little woman, five feet tall, raising, feeding, loving, clothing and housing five children. My mother was an angel to me.

By age five mother's influence paid off and I decided to try out for my brother Truman's little league baseball team, the Newton Braves. This was a big deal. Truman told me I was too young and not good enough to make it. Actually, he didn't want his little brother embarrassing him. However, like I am now, once someone tells me I cannot do a thing it powers me up and I go after it even harder. My oldest brother, Gary, who was my protector and believed in me, told me to try out. He said that I would be the best ball player in the family. It turned out I was too young and became the batboy for one year. At six I became a team player and at nine I was the captain of the team and a very good baseball player. I even made the Surrey All-Star team a number of times.

I sadly remember being called nigger at school. I can still hear this name in my mind. I remember my grade six teacher, telling the class to work like little niggers. Another incident I remember is being told by another teacher, at Bose Road Elementary School, that I could be the black sheep in a play we were doing. The racist atmosphere was thick in the school, but it never really got to me as mother always taught me that I was as good as or better than everyone and that I could do anything I put my mind to. Besides, those who crossed the line had to deal with one of the Green's or my mother who would go anywhere to protect her children.

As I grew older, if any kid called me nigger, I had gotten to the stage where I would throw a punch or two or three, even four, and I beat up several of these characters, who were also strapped because of their name calling. One principal I remember, Mr. Marcuzzi, was my guiding light and stood up for me if anyone called me a name. He also watched over my studies.

My older brothers and sisters, though they fought among themselves, always protected me and treated me like a little prince. As the youngest I was loved and cherished by mother and my siblings. So being poor and negro did not really mean that much to me. I grew up feeling strong and proud and just as good as anyone, and sometimes better. No challenge was too big for me.

Next in my story was the introduction of the saxophone, school bands and choirs. When I was twelve, my mother married a heavy-duty mechanic who earned good money. We moved into a very nice home in Fleetwood in North Surrey. I changed schools to Johnston Heights Elementary. I went to Johnston Heights Junior High School for grades 8, 9 and 10 and North Surrey Senior Secondary for grades 11 to 13.

On a September day in 1959, a wonderful music teacher entered my life. Don Murray introduced me to the alto saxophone. He said that the first time he saw me with a sax he knew it was an instrument that I was born to play. I joined band and was a band and choir member until I graduated from North Surrey High. However, it was not the sax alone that helped me mature. Don Murray was the key to my many successes in music and the only reason I did not drop out of school.

Don Murray was my mentor, referred to me as king, always treated me with respect and assured me that I could do and accomplish anything I set out to do. He was my surrogate father. As well as playing in the band I also joined the choir and sang solos in front of the entire school and at other community events. This experience and the numerous sports teams I joined such as basketball, soccer and baseball teams, gave me a great sense of pride, courage and accomplishment.

At age 14, however, I got hooked on high jumping. By age 15 I had beaten everyone my age in Surrey and in 1963 I traveled to the BC Junior Olympic Training Program Track and Field Championships in Vernon, BC. I was not on a track team, had no coach, no track suit, no spikes and no training program. However, I beat everyone and became the BC Junior Olympic Training Program High Jump Champion.

An interesting side bar here was what happened when I told my brother Truman that I could jump 5 feet 8 inches, which was, at that time, very high for a kid my age. He did not believe me. Well, to make a long one short, I took my brother to our outside clothesline and jumped it. That sealed his belief in my high jumping ability. The gold medal I won in Vernon was such a confidence builder. Newspaper articles, photos in the media and interviews followed.

I was five feet 10 inches tall, an accomplished singer, one of the top athletes and young musicians in my school and in the province. Well, I was flying high and could not have anticipated what was just around the corner.

I became very ill with a digestive tract problem and was hospitalized. However, along came my faith in myself, the support of my family and even my teachers. In fact my math teacher, Mr. Bury, came to our home to teach me math for several months. I thank Mr. Bury for this. After the year was up I was healed and healthy. Sadly I had lost my interest in sports and took up music as my one and only love.

At age eighteen I got another opportunity of a lifetime.

My older brother Truman was a singer in a rhythm and blues band called the Organization. The group needed another singer. I auditioned for the job. I became a singer in one of the biggest bands in the city. Singing solo, and in a group we called the Emotions, was incredible. We performed, all sixteen of us, in clubs, at universities and at numerous sports banquets. It was so cool performing Knock on Wood, My

Girl, Hold on I'm Coming, Try a Little Tenderness, Proud Mary and other covers of the day. Truman, who had been the lead singer, later quit the band and I became the lead.

I was in grade 11 and one day, while walking out of home room, I spotted the most beautiful girl I had ever seen. She was also the calmest and sweetest looking girl I had ever seen. It was love at first sight, for me at least. On spotting her, I told my friend Randy Gibbons that I was in love and would marry her some day. I didn't know her name but that did not matter. She was a cheerleader and the school's Valentine Queen. We finally met and became friends, though we did not date for some time. She graduated from North Surrey and went to SFU. I asked her out and two years later, in June 1969, we married. We were both 21 and this was the best day of my life. As of June 2007 we will have been married for 38 years.

We had a big problem before the wedding. Marlies' dad was against the marriage. We actually did not really care what her dad felt as we were madly in love. It was not our problem but his that created this situation. Sadly, none of her family attended our wedding.

It was 1969, we were living in the West End, I worked at Woodward's as a Section Head in Oakridge, and Marlies worked at an insurance company across the street. We lived the perfect love story. Lunches, walks along English Bay, cycling through Stanley Park, hours of tennis, swimming and romantic dinners. Love, Love, and more Love. I sang in a band called Gastown. We played in such clubs as Oilcan Harry's and The Daisy. Marlies came to every gig as we were inseparable.

I remember the band returning from a tour of the interior of BC. Once again life took a tragic turn.

It was a Sunday, 11:00 pm in the spring of 1970, when there was a knock at the door of our apartment on Barclay Street in the West End of Vancouver. You see, we did not have a telephone. When we opened the door, it was our landlord who said there was a call and it sounded serious. I got dressed and headed to his apartment. I picked up the phone and it was my brother Truman, who, on my hello, coldly said that someone shot and killed Jackie, our older sister. In shock, I left the apartment to tell Marlies. We were both crushed when the family arrived with the police close behind. They told us what had happened and the next day they arrested a known killer named Andy Bruce. He went to trial, was found guilty of first degree murder and jailed for 25 years. Surviving this tragedy, and all of the challenges mentioned in this book, prepared me to meet and beat any challenges life can throw at me.

At the time of my sister's murder I was a Section Head at Woodward's Oakridge. I had risen to this number three position in Boy's Wear after having worked there for just a few months. The death of our beloved 28 year old sister, at the hands of this killer, made me feel I had to do something that was far more meaningful. I decided to go to university. Problem was I had a low grade point average when I graduated high school. When I applied to Simon Fraser University, I was advised to go to VCC King Edward Campus and bring my academic marks up. Big challenge to overcome, as I was a poor reader and writer and did not know how I would make the grade. Well, my wife and mentor, Marlies was an excellent writer, reader, student and teacher and she spent long hours teaching me and improving my skills. After many grueling hours of hard work and concentration, I caught on and became a very

good student. I graduated from Langara College
with four As and one B and received a
scholarship to go to SFU.

Once again Marlies and I met the challenge and
proved that I could in fact do whatever I could
dream. Marlies, for sure, never doubted me and
gave me all the time and support I needed to
achieve my next goal.

After studying History, Political Science,
Sociology, Anthropology and English I decided
to become a teacher and was accepted into the
Professional Development Program. I graduated
in 1972 and accepted a position as a classroom
teacher at Ladner Elementary School in Delta,
BC. I was the head of the school band and music
program. I loved teaching, as it was exciting to
experience the successes of my students.

Not to leave out the most important part, we have
two daughters who have blessed our lives.

During this time Marlies returned to SFU and
finished her Professional Development Program
and acquired her teaching certificate. In 1981 I
left the elementary system and moved to the
junior secondary level. I joined the staff of

Tsawwassen Junior Secondary School and re-built the faltering music program. I established and taught bands and guitar groups and also conducted a community band part time. I was also the co-ordinator of the Arts Department.

I also joined the Board of Directors of the Vancouver based Paula Ross Dance Company and became the first president and manager of the Goh Ballet Society and Goh Ballet Dance Company.

In 1984, we rented a school from the Delta School Board and ran a Fine and Performing Arts School. I was the Executive Director and President of the Board of Directors. I was also a Director of the Tsawwassen Sun Festival Society. I was still singing part time in a band and teaching private music lessons. I was President of the Delta Arts Council and Vice-president of the Delta Music Teacher's Association. And to do even more for my community, I was on the Board of Directors of The Delta Junior Community Band Society.

As you could expect, my charmed life hit another snag and once again I was called on to be strong and climb another mountain. In 1984 I fell very ill with a digestive tract problem and was in the hospital off and on for six months.

Before this befell me, Marlies, at age 30, had started dance classes and progressed to where, at age 35 she auditioned and was accepted into the SFU Dance Degree Program. Marlies had to run the Arts Society and dance school while I was busy dying. She took a year off SFU, but with the help of some wonderful people, managed to return to the program and graduated with a BA in Dance. Again, the ultimate challenge to survive was on me and with the love of my wife and kids and friends and a great doctor, I survived. I had surgery and the illness ended.

The School Board election was very challenging. Once again I was told by many that as an Independent I did not stand a chance of getting elected. Traditionally, independents did not do well in Delta. As a black man, many told me my chances were even slimmer. Well, Marlies and I knew I could win. I had no experience in government at this time, but knew I wanted to help improve the education of students. I also had no experience at losing anything and entered to win, which I did. Of 15 candidates I came 6th out of the 7 to be elected. I was sworn in as an

Independent Trustee. My passion and advocacy was for the Arts.

I hosted my own cable TV show called The Stage of the Arts and produced a television public service announcement with the late John Candy as the host. Marlies floor directed this program. I went back to teaching in Richmond and Vancouver and I loved it.

In 1992 I co-created, with James Barber, The Urban Peasant cooking series. Marlies and I became the Executive Producer and Creative Producer, respectively, of this successful cooking series. This series was broadcast in 120 countries.

I raised all of the cash for the production, oversaw all aspects of the production, set up the sales of the Urban Peasant book, enlisted and managed the distributor in the US and managed the company. I negotiated all contracts, including our production contract with the CBC which was the first broadcaster of the series. Marlies was responsible for the creative elements of the program along with our Director Lawrence McDonald.

James Barber, whom CBC said could not be turned into a television show host, turned out to be wonderful on camera. However he did spend much of his time demanding more money, missing cues, hitting on female hosts who were half his age and having to be checked for some of the crazy things he said on air. In 1993 I called James on my cell phone and told him I could not and would not deal with his crazy behaviour any longer. I quit the show. Barber was forced to buy me out. Later we will deal with the story Barber told the media when he was asked by Vision Vancouver to slam me.

Next I worked on producing some TV pilots and programs and a television special called Catch the Step that aired on BCTV. I also produced a television commercial, starring Alexander Mogilny, for a new hockey stick that the NHL endorsed. I also produced a pilot for a proposed television series called Chef on the Run hosted by former Olympians Diane and Doug Clement.

I also produced and hosted a pilot for a sports series called Sports Star Challenge. On this program I interviewed, worked out with and challenged world class athletes to their sport. I spent time with Lou Passaglia of the BC Lions,

Brian Hill and Stu Jackson of the Grizzlies. I participated in batting practice with the Vancouver Canadians. I challenged and raced Robert Esmie, a member of the Atlanta 1996 Donovan Bailey Canadian Olympic gold medal 4 x 100 relay team.

So we are at 2002 when I met a representative from KCTS Television in Seattle, and was asked to raise $3mil. US for their production unit. Not shying away from any challenge, I raised the money. I also became marketer and Co-Executive Producer of the nine programs KCTS was to produce, including Bill Nye the Science Guy's new series called The Eyes of Nye.

For two years after this I worked at home and in office space supplied by my friend and well-known producer Blair Reekie. I took on several marketing contracts. Life with my wife and kids was great. We now arrive at 2003 and my decision to run for Mayor.

Me in Grade One – My mother's Little Prince (do I really need to circle my face?). Bose Road Elementary, Newton, Surrey.

This is my favourite picture of me and my older brother Truman in our home in Newton. The visible wear and tear on the wall isn't all due to an aging photo.

This is me at the Newton Braves year-end baseball banquet. To my right is my brother Truman and Bobbie Wilson. Behind us, on the left, is the Manager of the then Vancouver Mounties Team and to his right is Mr. Baseball.

Me, high jumping at age 15. Check out the high-tech gear! In this outfit, I went on to win a gold medal in the Junior Olympic Training Program Championships in Vernon, BC (1963).

I'm the skinny guy on the right in the singing group The Emotions, part of the R&B Band, The Organization (about 1966).

Marlies and I, and a guy whose name I can't remember, modeled for the Viking Hair Salon's advertising campaign. When released as a bus ad, we followed it around Vancouver (1969).

My mother is in the back on the far left. My Aunt Adele is on the far right. My cousin Ivan is the boy in front on the left and my half sister Gertrude is the young girl on the far right. The lady seated is my mother and aunt's stepmother (approx. 1944).

My mother Annie today.

My stepdad, Gordie taken in the
1950's in Downtown Vancouver.

My band at Port Guichon Elementary School in Ladner
(1980/81).

Conducting my first Secondary School Band Concert at
Tsawwassen Jr. Secondary (approx. 1982).

This was my student's and my favourite conducting
picture. Tsawwassen Jr. Secondary School, Delta (1984).

Me, Marlies and our two daughters, Erin and Arlana, attend the Lt. Governor's Garden Party given by His Honour Robert G. Rogers (back row on the right) (1984).

Delta School Board inaugural meeting December 1, 1987.

The Green Family

CHAPTER FOUR

My life has been filled with achieving every dream I have dreamed. The people I have known have supported me in all things and there has been no mountain I could not climb. I have made mistakes, as it is normal to do if one is, in fact, human. Yet, I can rest assured that these mistakes have taught me a great deal. My life experiences have most importantly taught me how to be a leader and how to be led. My charmed life, I felt, prepared me to be Mayor of Vancouver.

This is why Jim Green's version, that I ran to confuse voters and jumped into the race at the last moment, always seemed so off the mark. I had told people I was running for Mayor before there was a Vision Vancouver, before Larry Campbell announced that he had decided not to seek another term as Mayor of Vancouver and long before Jim Green announced his candidacy.

Proof, we have proof. John at Black Dog Video on Cambie Street in Vancouver wrote to me in January 2007. There were no last minute decisions to run for Mayor as has been widely reported.

JOHN SKIBINSKI
303-1918 Haro Street,
Vancouver, BC, V6G 1H6

January 19, 2007

Dear James,

As I told you a while back, I've actually had to defend you from people who claim that you ran for mayor to confuse voters and help elect Sam Sullivan.

I tell them about you coming into Black Dog Video, where I work, in the spring of 2003 and telling me that you were going to run for Mayor and that you felt you could beat Larry Campbell.

I think this clearly shows that you were planning to run for mayor long before Jim Green had any idea that he would be entering the race. We both know this is true, and I hope this statement is helpful.

Anyway, if voters were even minimally informed about the election they would have been able to differentiate between James Green and Jim Green.

Regards,

John Skibinski

Why Run?

Another motivator for me in 2003 was an article written by Sandy McCormick in The Province Newspaper on Thursday, March 20, 2003 (in case you want the full article). Sandy McCormick stated that Mayor Larry Campbell and COPE were on a spending spree that would result in long-term financial problems for the taxpayers of the city. She cited that Larry had promised to hold any tax hikes to 3.9%, but city staff estimated that, to maintain the services, the hike would have to go as high as 5.5%.

McCormick pointed out Larry and COPE's $5.5mil. purchase of Woodward's, $200,000 housing for squatters, a Peace Committee cost of $25,000, an Olympic after-the-fact poll of $600,000, $20,000 studies of mass transit to Richmond, $150,000 annually to open the downtown library year-round, and two funds of $100,000; one to subsidize youth access to community and sports facilities and a second for cultural endeavours. McCormick wondered, as I did, where Larry planned to get the money from, as the increased taxes would have left a shortfall of $22,000,000. Overall, McCormick concluded that Larry's spending was beyond what taxpayers could afford and would have to be capped if he was to remember his promise to the taxpayers of Vancouver.

Jim Green and his Vision Vancouver team all voiced that I was a fraud, put there by Sam Sullivan at the last minute to confuse voters. With this in mind, they conjured up a number of strategies to get me off the ballot. To their dismay, I was not going anywhere.

I decided to challenge whomever would be running for Mayor of Vancouver. So many people have asked me why I did not run for council, school board or parks board first. Simple answer is, I was primed and ready to be Mayor and strongly felt, as I do now, that my destiny was to be the Mayor of Vancouver.

Besides, it was inconceivable for me to go for any other position as I was only interested in being the leader of this city. This position, I felt, was most suitable to my skill level. I had been a school trustee, sat on numerous boards and understood the limitations of being a director rather than a chairperson. I had been a committee member and now it was time to go for the top job. The thought of running for Mayor was exciting and fit very nicely with the challenges I had always loved beating. As Mayor I felt I could facilitate action in areas that had been neglected for years. I wanted to tackle such areas as social housing, business property tax reduction, a war on criminal predators, building treatment centres, women's protective and assistance programs, and reduction of the sex trade; as well as reform what I saw as an ineffective and dysfunctional city council. Most important, I felt the city needed a new business and fiscal approach.

In 2004 I went to a council meeting at city hall at 12th and Cambie to further research the job. When I arrived at the council chamber on the 3rd floor, I was met by Allen Garr, a reporter for the Vancouver Courier Newspaper. Garr seemed to challenge my right to be there with a "what are you doing here?" I answered that I was running for Mayor in November 2005, was doing research and that I would win with the million dollars I planned to raise. Garr seemed shocked and intrigued. All he said was "really" and "good luck".

I was researching the Mayor's job but, more importantly, I wanted to find out what I could do to help the people of the city. Therefore, I called councillor Jim Green and met with him. Jim

Green was someone I had admired. He was known as the defender of the poor and needy of the Downtown Eastside of Vancouver, the worst ghetto in Canada. We met and got along very well. He directed me to my first level of possible involvement in the city, his failed Four Corners Bank, which he hoped I could help save. This bank, Jim said, was essential for the people of the Downtown Eastside. The bank, of which Jim was President and CEO, allowed the poor to cash their welfare cheques and not fall prey to money lenders and other predators such as violent drug users. It gave them hope and pride to have a bank account. Jim and a social planner at city hall set up a meeting with city administrators such as the head of finance and some officials from the provincial government. In the final analysis I walked away from this money losing venture as it had reportedly already lost $5,000,000 of taxpayer's money.

Remember, Jim Green commented many times during the election that I had never been to city hall. So who was I meeting with in his office when I met with a councillor Jim Green? Who was I meeting with at city hall when I met with a councillor Jim Green and a number of City Hall staff to discuss strategies to save the Four Corners

Bank? Did Jim Green have a clone, or a twin brother with the same name?

The bank was dead, but I met with others to see where I might help the city. Several meetings took place and I decided to walk away from city hall for the time being as I felt they had made a business out of poverty and were not making any progress in solving the problems of the people in the Downtown Eastside of Vancouver. I also felt, like I do today, that the city was being poorly governed. I felt that the status quo had to be broken in order for positive change to be made.

This experience with civic government left a bad taste in my mouth and, in fact, further motivated me to run for Mayor. I felt this position would afford me the opportunity to get something done. I went back to my business endeavours.

Going in, I had no doubt that I could win the Mayor's chair. Why you ask? Firstly, my life has been like a university or prep school for this position. I had, and have, the qualities and experience to lead this city. I have seldom lost any competition I have entered. Like mother says, "Jimmy, you are a natural leader."

I was convinced that Larry Campbell, when I made his record clear to voters, would lose to me as he really had accomplished very little as Mayor. I felt once voters understood they had been misinformed about taxes they would revolt against Larry. I remembered George Bush Senior's "Read my Lips" line and his resulting loss. Surely Vancouver voters would punish Larry the same way for breaking the same promise. I felt this way until Larry was out and Jim Green was in. I felt that if I could beat Larry, Jim Green, with his bad behaviour and record, would be even more beatable.

Once Jim Green announced his candidacy, I felt voters would reject him because of his alignment with developers and his penchant for distorting the truth, suing people and bullying all who opposed him. I felt I could win as I had all of the bases covered and was not a member of the old guard. I had an excellent platform, message and vision for the city. I felt I could win because I felt the voters would reject Vision's pretense at being a middle of the road party. I felt that voters would not elect a former American draft dodger who spent a great deal of time losing taxpayer's money.

I felt that if Sam Sullivan or Christy Clark ended up being the NPA's candidate, I could beat either one, as Christy had a poor record as a minister in the provincial government and she did not live in Vancouver. However, she lost and I had Sam to think about. I felt I could beat Sam Sullivan as he had gained the least number of votes in the previous civic election and he had not been a real leader or champion of anything other than the anti ward campaign he led. I also learned he had an albatross around his neck that many felt would sink his ship. Once voters knew of Sam Sullivan's alleged criminal behaviour of buying drugs for addicts, I thought voters would reject him. I saw Sam Sullivan as a weak leader, who would not excite the voters or capture their imaginations as their new Mayor. I just could not see Sam or Jim attacking and solving the many serious challenges the city faced.

I thought that the voters would reject both of these men. Neither one was dynamic, articulate or energetic. They lacked charisma and the necessary leadership skills. I felt the city wanted another kind of Mayor and, once the media put me up against these guys, the voters would reject them and their records. Their infighting and confrontation at the council table would hurt them. I felt the city was tired of the dysfunctional council lead by Larry Campbell and comprised of Jim Green, Sam Sullivan and others. I knew that poverty, crime, taxes, homelessness and transportation were not under control. In fact, things were getting worse. I knew pollution was worse, traffic congestion downtown was bad, the police department, due to a deficiency in numbers, was struggling. Lastly, I believed that the money I could raise to finance television ads, newspaper ads and a massive flyer drop would put me in front of all opponents for the Mayor's job. I felt that the media would give me equal time, consideration and coverage in my bid for the city's top job.

I could not imagine Larry, Sam, or Jim as this city's next Mayor. Going in, and as the campaign progressed, I felt winning this was very possible.

I was ready to do battle and win the war and quite frankly I didn't know what I was in for. Even as I write this book, I am still somewhat surprised at what made the cast of characters play the game the way they did. In retrospect, my meetings at City Hall with Jim Green and others meant one thing; he obviously saw me as an intelligent, articulate and successful businessman. I have no doubt Jim believed I was very well off. In the media I was quoted as saying I planned to spend thousands of dollars on my campaign. Now I understand that Jim saw me as a real threat to his dream. Once I told him I was running for Mayor, he realized he might have trouble beating me and he saw me as a viable candidate who had to be stopped at any cost. Jim offered me the opportunity to run with Vision Vancouver if I would give up running for Mayor.

CHAPTER FIVE

Who is Jim Green?

When I first met him at city hall in 2004, Jim presented himself as a person who cared first and foremost about people, not power. I am sure this was true until he smelled power when Vision Vancouver was formed and Larry Campbell decided not to run for Mayor and anointed Jim as the next Caesar. He seemed to feel that the Mayor's chair was his by divine right. Jim illustrated that he believed the end justified his means even if that meant smearing the reputation of his opponents; including Silent Sam, James Green or anyone who represented a threat to his rise to power.

Also, Jim seems to lack a sense of humour. The Courier newspaper printed my joke answer to a question whether Jim and I were related. In the September 7, 2005 issue, Jim responded with a recent family history which he felt would dispel the notion that we may be related through an ancestral slave owner scenario. Jim, it was a JOKE. Right in the article it was reported as James Green's JOKE.

I feel this man would be a perfect fit for Mayor of some small southern town, just not Vancouver. Seriously, Jim Green did not and never will fit the bill the people of Vancouver have for their Mayor; as shown by his previous defeat in his bid for the Mayorship. Throughout the campaign numerous people told me Jim believes that this city is his domain and anyone who challenges him is his enemy and an enemy of the people.

To give you some idea of Jim's financial history, let's review:

1. The bank of which Jim Green was President and CEO reportedly lost over $5mil. of taxpayers' money.

2. Jim Green, Larry Campbell and COPE promised taxpayers that taxes would be kept at the same rate as inflation, which was 2%. COPE, under Larry Campbell and Jim Green, caused a tax increase in the area of 6%.

3. The Woodward's deal, which Jim Green negotiated with the developers, resulted in a $32mil. shortfall of which the taxpayers would have to pay $13mil. As well, Jim Green negotiated an interest free loan for the developers that would allow the developers to buy the Woodward's project from the City. A

sizeable investment by Vancouver taxpayers, but without any participation in the profit side of the venture. Be clear, Jim Green is a developer, negotiated with developers on behalf of the City and accepted campaign contributions from developers. This is called, in all precincts, political corruption. Jim says that's the way things are done in this city.

4. Jamie Lee Hamilton has alleged financial misconduct on behalf of Jim Green. This is before the courts, as Jim Green is suing Jamie Lee Hamilton for her accusations.

5. Jim Green, and others of Vision, left COPE with a large debt in the area of $300,000 when the two parties split.

6. Jim Green accepted a donation of $170,000, and the contributor who made the donation has been arrested by the FBI as of 2007.

7. Jim Green's party had a $157,000 campaign debt after the 2005 campaign.

In a recent newspaper article, Jim stated that Vision decided to take the highest road they possibly could with their campaign. If their behaviour was the high road, I would hate to experience their low road. I would have actually have needed the bullet proof vest I joked about during the campaign.

As well as the above, Jim made many negative references in the media about my candidacy as did his cohorts in Vision. Remember, this is the man who called on me to save his Four Corners Bank, who I met several times and who had invited me to run with Vision Vancouver.

As you will read later, Jim also made many attempts to have me barred from All Candidates Meetings. This information was supplied to me by Charlie Smith of the Georgia Straight. High road?

Speaking to Raymond Louie, a Vision candidate for council, and a relatively good but misguided councillor, I said that Vision might be okay and may do well except for one thing; they had the wrong candidate for Mayor in Jim Green. I told Raymond that Jim Green was a major liability to the team. Whatever I said about Jim Green, Vision may have realized I was right. What I said might have heightened their attempts to discredit me. Like it or not, this guy would never be Mayor of Vancouver due to his liabilities. Let's delve into Jim Green a little deeper.

We should all admit to ourselves here that Jim, Larry and COPE gained power in part because the NPA did such a poor job. It was not because of the wonderfulness of Larry and Jim. As a result, Jim was elected a councillor even though he had lost two bids for election, one for Mayor and one for MLA, prior to 2002.

It is generally thought that Jim Green was still working for the DTES of Vancouver during the 2005 election, when in reality he was working for developers.

He left the Downtown Eastside Residents Association in 1990. He has served one term as a councillor and still perpetuates the myth that he has continued his work to help the people there, which he has not. Jim has been a developer and, as a councillor, negotiated the Woodward's deal with developers. He has had his election expenses paid for by developers and now, after losing the election, is employed by a development company. During the election, at an All Candidates Meeting, I asked Jim if he did not see any conflict and he stated proudly that that's the way we do things in Vancouver.

To my surprise, and I learned this in March 2006, Jim and Vision spent $1.5mil. on their campaign and couldn't sell their brand to the voters of Vancouver. But I am getting ahead of myself.

Former Mayor Philip Owen had his say about Jim Green in an article published in the Vancouver Sun on Monday, November 14, 2005. One quote from the article states Jim Green is "a political freeloader" who has "done nothing but line up at the public trough his whole life". He goes on to COPE taking credit for what Philip claims the NPA started. To cap it all off Philip is reported as saying, "Jim Green has never put any of his money into a business or created jobs. He doesn't understand money".

With all of this, I realized that Jim lost his way. Power, or the lust for power, can corrupt.

CHAPTER SIX

Who is Sam Sullivan?

At the time of the 2005 election, Sam had already been on council for four terms. Sam had learned how to win elections and had a large following in the city. Sam has a very humble and engaging quality about him. He knows how to use his challenges to his advantage and how to speak to and satisfy the wishes of the well off, the developers and other haves in this city. As of January 2007, Sam is not seen as a good or relevant Mayor by many. Even his own party members are attacking him.

Sam has been called a made man, driven by his team and wealthy supporters. Sam has overcome much adversity in his life. Unfortunately, Sam is not a leader and cannot actually chair a council meeting properly. Sam has no overall plan for the city. He has no well thought-out plan to solve the city's serious problems. During the campaign he really did not say much that had any depth. To win, he didn't have to. He just capitalized on the dislike so many had for Jim Green and Jim's mean spirited, condescending and arrogant manner; as well as his feeling of entitlement.

In the context of the campaign Sam must have read the *Art of War* by Sun Zhu, as he used many of the key strategies in this book. The number one strategy of Sam and his gang of spin doctors was to paint Sam as weak, draw the enemy in and then cut off his head. This worked so often against Jim Green that it was laughable. I saw Jim leave many All Candidates Meetings very upset, as Jim seldom understood the power and treachery of Sam and, in fact, Jim always underestimated Sam. This became clear to me after one All Candidates Meeting. The two of them showed their true colours acting like little boys fighting over a Tonka Toy. I quickly lost respect for Sam and Jim. I also learned that Sam would come up with any platform, possible or not, if he thought it would gain votes.

During his term on council, when COPE was in the majority, he spent much time voting against motions - good or bad - as long as COPE had made the motion. Currently, he is spending his time dismantling anything that Larry Campbell, Jim Green or COPE put in place.

After the election, and during Citizen's Day, I decided to go to City Hall and meet Sam, as other citizens were doing. We talked about crime and he gave me a book and signed it *"To James Green, the man whose job I took"*. This one meeting triggered Vision to tell others I often visited Sam at City Hall. Once again, one visit becomes often; like one telephone call becomes a conspiracy.

The divisiveness Sam displays at the council table is bad for the city and will hurt Sam come next election.

Now, to be fair, after repeating the Sun article regarding Philip Owen's take on Jim Green, here is Larry Campbell's take on Sam Sullivan. I must say I can't disagree with him. Such things as, "The NPA didn't like him. They buried him for nine years. He doesn't know a thing about running government". Larry goes on to relate the story of Sam supplying drugs to a survival sex-trade worker and supplying money to watch a drug deal go down. "You know what it goes to: Good judgment and common sense. And that's what you need to be Mayor and Sam has neither of those".

CHAPTER SEVEN

Who is Larry Campbell?

The man on the throne, and the man supposedly behind Jim Green during the election, was Larry Campbell. Larry has to take responsibility for the negative and confrontational atmosphere and dysfunctional state of civic government in Vancouver from 2002 to 2005. Unfortunately, Jim Green, if elected Mayor, would have continued Larry's negative legacy.

When Larry was elected it was not a vote for COPE and Larry, but a vote against the NPA. When Sam and the NPA won in 2005, it was not a vote for the NPA but a vote against COPE, Vision, Jim Green and Larry Campbell.

I have never met Larry Campbell, so I can only base my take on what others have said about him, his record, how he responded to my campaign and how he spoke about me after the campaign. I do know that Larry was a cop and a coroner and that he certainly did not use any investigative skills to find out for himself if what Vision was saying about me was true or false. Or did he?

Perhaps Vancouver Sun's Barbara Yaffe's column about Larry's appointment to the Canadian Senate clearly opens a window to who Larry Campbell is.

Take it away Ms. Yaffe
> "As for Larry Campbell, the appointment stinks. Campbell, Vancouver's Mayor of 2 1/2 years, who has said of himself "I'm not a politician," is not a politician. . . .

> "In fact, he's a foulmouthed, testy man who wasn't at all receptive to anyone who didn't share his views."

This column showed Larry and Vision were vulnerable to defeat.

Then there was the televised meeting where Larry called protesters losers and told them to get a job. When you add to this the media moment where Larry called the American Bush-appointed 'drug czar' an idiot who doesn't know what he's talking about, you will see what spurred me on further to run for Mayor.

Vancouver voters were somewhat taken with the Da Vinci's Inquest television program. It made Larry somewhat of a local hero/celebrity. This program somehow elevated Larry to a level far beyond what Larry deserves or can live up to.

Larry and Jim played a big role in breaking up COPE. When they left and formed Vision, they allegedly left COPE with a sizable debt in the hundreds of thousands of dollars. Walking away from this debt, which they incurred to win in 2002, is outrageous and even more so as they allegedly left it entirely in the hands of COPE's David Cadman to repay.

Then there is the alleged theft of COPE's membership list by Vision Vancouver. This list is protected by solemn privacy laws and is the sole responsibility of COPE to protect and use to communicate with long standing COPE members. The alleged theft of this list is not only a violation of the privacy of 30,000 voters, but a heinous criminal act designed to undermine a political opponent. US president Richard Nixon could not have planned a better covert action.

Larry's acceptance of a seat in the Canadian Senate, with the Liberals, puts another nail in the coffin of his reputation. This did not surprise many who really knew Larry. Think about it: NDP backed, Vision Vancouver middle-of-the-road party leader jumps in bed with the ailing Liberals to gain a cozy well-paid retirement job in the Canadian Senate.

Also, Larry lives in somewhat of a dream world. At one of his Mayor's forums he stated that crystal meth was not at the epidemic stage. Larry, as the leader of this city, should have known that any comment that trivializes how much pain meth has caused our citizens is inappropriate and lacks good sense and sound leadership.

When asked what he was most proud of as Mayor by Global's Deborah Hope, Larry said, "Completing the Four Pillar's Program". I have some news for you Larry, one injection site does not constitute a completed program. It was Phillip Owen's baby, and Larry really hadn't much to do with it.

The best window to the soul of this man is his outburst at Liberal Headquarters when he called me a criminal. No proof of anything, no conversation with me ever, no crime ever committed, nothing criminal on my record; yet the former cop and coroner passed sentence on me because his boy lost the election. And the best part of it is that when he was asked by media if he had called me a criminal he said he didn't. He claimed he merely said that I do not pay my bills in a timely manner. Imagine the scenario. Larry Campbell, known for his bad temper and abusive mouth, is speaking with Mark Marissen at the Liberal Headquarters in Vancouver. I arrive. Larry spots me and storms down a hallway. Mark Marissen, the head Liberal organizer for BC, goes to calm Larry down. Larry points at me in his anger and says "get rid of James Green. He doesn't pay his bills in a timely manner!" Next Larry storms out of the building. Is this believable given his history of verbally abusing others?

Larry is a very popular guy and was a very popular Mayor who ruled council with his loud voice, his aggression and his rather dirty mouth.

After reviewing Larry's record, behaviour, and unfulfilled promises, I think Larry figured it out: A strong candidate could take him out.

Remember, this is a man with a huge ego and losing would not be an option. So he made a deal with the Liberals to take a Senate seat and move over for Christy Clark to run. I believe Larry, deep down, knew Jim Green could not win. His whole act, that I was such a fraud, the stories he planted and his outrage when Jim did not win, was a smoke screen for his real agenda. His real agenda was to step down, split the left-leaning COPE and open the doors for the Liberal's Christy Clarke, Liberal boss Mark Marissen's wife. The fly in the otherwise perfect ointment was Sam. No one should be surprised at this as it fits Larry's M.O. In summary, I have no proof of this theory, but let's face it, Larry is capable of almost anything.

CHAPTER EIGHT

What It Would Take For Me To Win

By now you know that I had run a campaign at the civic level and had won as an Independent in Delta. In doing so I learned a great deal about how to win and how to run a campaign.

There are five basic things candidates for Mayor must have to win an election:

1. Voters must be able to picture you as the Mayor. Your meter, voice, dress, looks, speech and charisma must fit the majority of the voters' vision of what they want their Mayor to be.

2. You must have a large and dedicated team of volunteers, campaign experts and fundraisers; and a campaign manager who knows the ropes.

3. You must have an appealing message and you must get your message out.

4. The media must give you continuing and extensive coverage.

5. You must have the money to buy television time, radio time and newspaper and magazine

space; as well as for flyers and brochures to distribute to all homes in the city.

So what did I have going for me?

Going into the race I felt I was in good shape. I had experience at the civic level, I am articulate, my family has roots in the city that date back to 1935, I am not bad looking, relatively charismatic and have contacts in many areas of the city. My 20 years as an educator and arts administrator and executive producer, conductor, athlete and coach represented my leadership ability and experience. I had been founder and president of arts organizations and a community leader. I had as much experience or more than Larry Campbell when he ran for Mayor and won. No other candidate for Mayor, except Sam Sullivan, had more civic experience than me. There was no doubt in my mind that those who met me and talked to me would have the image in their minds that I could be Mayor. In fact, many said during the campaign that I looked like I should be the Mayor of Vancouver.

Message-wise, Jim's was negative and attacking. As his financial disclosures now show, Jim Green was backed by big money and was a point man for powerful groups in the city. As Mayor he would have been a disaster as he knows nothing of fiscal responsibility, flexibility, and fairness.

Message-wise, Sam really doesn't have a message beyond generalizations. He has no action strategies and no implementation programs. Sam, like Jim Green, represents the powerful and the wealthy of this city. Sam, like Jim, is a kept politician who adheres to party line and not to the needs of the voters and citizens of Vancouver.

Jim Green, on the charisma side of the equation, did not have much going for him. I don't care what you say, people want their leaders to at least appear stately. During the campaign, a number of people reported to me that they had seen Jim Green less than distinguished at various events such as the Vancouver Film Festival.

Jim had only one three year term at the civic level as a councillor. I have a feeling Larry was a figurehead who kissed babies, drank with the boys, smoked his face off, attended lots of events, schmoozed the media, held some forums and chaired council meetings like Genghis Khan. Jim did the dirty work. They were the bad guy/bad

guy team and it blew up in their cigar-smoking
faces.

I had been to council meetings and seen them
function, or in the case of the Larry Campbell
council, dysfunction. Believe me, there was no
love at the city council table. In fact, I have not
seen such an inept group as the COPE / Vision /
NPA council, then and now. I was sure Jim Green
did not have what it takes to be a drum majorette,
let alone a Mayor.

So the idea that I could be Mayor was a done deal
in my mind. Certainly, on the image side of
things, I had all opponents beat. Jim Green and
Sam Sullivan were the same-old same old. They
were, in my view, part of the problem and I was
the solution.

The Big Advertising Firm
In DDB Canada I had the support of one of the
top marketing and advertising companies in the
country. Frank Palmer, the president of this
company, had committed to supporting me. His
company, DDB, has an impressive client list and
reputation. The following email, sent to me by
Frank Palmer, attests to this commitment.

Frank and I had met on other business and he believed that I could win. He had his team create campaign materials based on the slogan "Be Heard". It was brilliant and would have undoubtedly helped put me over the top.

Email From Frank Palmer
To James Green
> Thursday August 25, 2005 7:42am
> Yes I will support you. I said that we would do the layouts/design for your campaign, newspapers, buttons, lawn signs, etc. You'll need to get someone to pay for the final printing and screening etc. We are not in a position to financially help. When do you announce?

So this meant DDB would prepare everything for printing and screening and I would only need a printer. I had hoped that Bob Faulkner, the manager of Metropolitan Fine Printers, would do the job. I thought it was good news that Palmer and Faulkner knew each other. Before I get to this next email let me tell you something about Frank Palmer, because he is one of the best and his faith in me surely enhanced my belief that I could and would be Mayor.

With DDB on board I would have had thousands of flyers, posters, signs and other valuable materials laid out free of charge.

Frank Palmer
I found the following information about Frank Palmer on the internet.

> As founder of Palmer Jarvis and engineer of the 1995 Palmer Jarvis /DDB merger, Frank is a well-respected member of Canada's advertising community. Under his direction, Palmer Jarvis DDB has become one of Canada's largest advertising agencies, earning many Agency of the Year honours from the country's leading industry publications along the way, while jealously maintaining its entrepreneurial, innovative and thought provoking reputation. Frank's primary responsibilities include new business development opportunities.

Following is the relevant part of an email from DDB executive, Dean Ellisat, that changed everything and reversed Frank Palmer's commitment.

From Dean Ellisat
To James Green
Wednesday October 05, 2005 11:39 AM
> One important point I need to broach with you is the workload expectation at this point. In speaking with our studio design group, we are in a position to continue to move forward and prepare final artwork elements for the above mentioned campaign items. However, we're currently crunched for time with our current client workload and will need to re-consider the depth of our involvement in the additional materials you requested (newspaper ads, television graphics, business card, and signs-up card) with special note to the 10 page policy book.
>
> As outlined in your earlier conversation with Frank and subsequent email from Bill, by all accounts, we're not in a position at this time to go much deeper than

providing the initial tagline and artwork files for the poster, lawn sign and flyer within the pro-bono arrangement. With that said, what we can offer you beyond the initial elements will have to be strictly on a paid-for basis.

Following tomorrow's presentation, we would need to quote based on our project management time, further design time and any production hard costs through our vender partners. This will hopefully allow us to find a balance between our time and your needs.
Dean Ellisat
Group Account Manager
DDB Canada

A few days later I received an estimate for $16,575 for design, layout and other costs. I did not understand this estimate as it was in opposition to what I had been promised by Frank Palmer. They were to prepare everything for production and now they submitted a cost estimate I was supposed to pay.

At the end of the day Frank Palmer and DDB were out of the campaign. Frank's loss as a supporter hurt me greatly.

The Printer

I met Bob Faulkner of Metropolitan Fine Printers in 1998, when I was developing a television series called Sports Star Challenge. I wanted to include Bob as a guest on the series. We got along very well. The point here is, I met Bob long before the 2005 election and knew that he managed a large printing company. So, my friends and enemies, it was not strange that I called Bob to be my printer. Until Bob told me, during the campaign, I did not know he even knew Sam Sullivan. However, it is not strange for me to know Bob, Bob to know Sam and for me not to know Sam knew Bob. Vancouver is a small pond and many of the fish, big and small, know each other.

In kind is as good as cash. I had planned well and felt I likely had a printer to do the work Frank would have prepared for me. I had attempted to connect with Bob Faulkner, but he was too busy for about a month. Finally we met. I told him what I needed and he said he would do it. However, to my surprise, he told me he knew

Sam Sullivan and would have to call Sam to be
sure it was alright with him. I got a call from Bob
a few days later. He said he was very sorry, but
Sam had said no and he did not want to hurt Sam.
I lost my advertising company and printer in one
fell swoop.

On the one hand the press said Sam Sullivan
made an office-related phone call to help me; on
the other hand Sam stops Bob Faulkner from
doing my printing. Where does it stop? Strange
and somewhat ridiculous if you ask me. Having
these elements intact would have made a great
difference in my exposure to all of Vancouver. If
I had the materials Frank and Bob would have
supplied, my chances would have been much
better.

The Infamous Office
Having a campaign office was another plus. I was
so happy and proud to have an office in the Plaza
of Nations. This office obviously gave Sam and
Jim the jitters, and it showed my campaign was
real and strong. I could never have anticipated the
controversy it would cause.

The office was fully equipped with computer,
board room, two offices and a full circle set of

glass windows where we put large signs that read 'Vote James Green for Mayor'. Large pictures of me were a part of this display. The office was on the walkway along the seawall south of the Plaza of Nations. Anyone who passed the area saw my pictures and signs. The Azure owners, Duro and Julius, invited me to many events at their restaurant and I was introduced to hundreds as the next Mayor of Vancouver. I met hundreds of people there and numerous people dropped into the office to talk. Some students from BCIT taped an interview at the office. A Vancouver Sun photographer took pictures just outside of the office.

I held meetings there as well. I did not know Sam Sullivan. Actually, I expected Christy Clark would be the candidate for the NPA and that Sam would not be a factor. Of course, I was wrong. It must be understood that I was installed in this space long before the outcome of the NPA race for Mayor was settled and Sam was victorious. I got the office because my friend Joe, whom I had known for five years, knew Duro.

Duro made all the decisions regarding my use of the space. Julius Simon, the man a CTV reporter interviewed, did not negotiate the space with me.

As I said, who would move into this space if they were involved in any form of collusion with Sam Sullivan or the NPA?

CHAPTER NINE

Show Me The Money

With supporters like Dennis Law, the owner of the Centre in Vancouver for Performing Arts, I thought I had a major contributor. Dennis, I felt, would supply a great deal of money as we had many meetings on various business deals and he seemed to be committed. However, from the email below it became clear he was frightened off and I had lost a major contributor. The following left me shocked and bewildered.

Dennis Law to James Green
Sunday October 23, 2005
Hi Jim

> Your being Mayor is better than the other alternatives, but I have been repeatedly warned by people in the "know" that I must not overtly take sides in these political matters, especially when no party will clearly win.

Dennis Law did offer to give me a percentage of the gate from one of his performances at the Centre in Vancouver, based on the number of tickets I sold. My campaign manager dropped the ball on this as well.

Fundraising

Candidates raise money or have fundraisers to do this for them. "So, if this is true," you ask, "how come you could not raise the thousands of dollars you needed to run the campaign?" Firstly, as mentioned above, Dennis Law was frightened off or warned at least, not to support me.

Many said they would support me with small donations, but the big money people never materialized. Next, an acquaintance, Nizar, said he would help. He then told me he had been threatened. He said that he did not come to Canada to be threatened and he bought $2800 worth of ads in an Indo Canadian newspaper for my campaign. Then there was the fundraiser I was planning at Azure. The Azure staff kept mixing up my timing, menu and budget. Due to the Azure staff's ineptness no event was ever held, which also speaks to my belief that Sam's so called friend Julius was not helping me, or I would have had my fundraiser at the Azure. Therefore, my means of raising money was left to me making calls to people directly.

I contacted some so-called important people such as Glen Clark, the former BC Premier, who now worked for Jimmy Pattison, and who was taking care of requests for contributions. Glen Clark was friendly, but the runaround I received did not surprise me. He said he would have to talk to Jimmy and that Jimmy was out of the country. I was to call him back in two weeks, and I did. He was out and his assistant said he would get back to me in a couple of days.

Glen took a great deal of time to get back to me. Glen was a questionable premier and he was not forthright this time either. I knew, and he knew, that I would get no support from the Pattison Group. In fact, when I finally did reach Glen after, say, five calls to his office, he gave me the bad news ... No.

SIDE BAR HERE. Glen did go on to speak at length about the signage laws in Vancouver and the rule allowing only three newspaper boxes per corner. Was this to put a bug in my ear just in case I did end up with some useful authority? Just like Glen, always hedging his bets.

I went on to call other power brokers in the city to tell them I was running and in some cases to see if there was any support. I called or emailed Peter Wall, Edgar Kaiser, Gordon Campbell, Carol James, Lorne Mayencourt, Leonard George, Matt Vickers, Kevin Evans and many others. No luck there. The most supportive Mayencourt was Lorne's brother who offered to put up my signs in his neighbourhood and on his car lot.

The Dal Richards' Story
Dal Richards, I am sure, is a wonderful man. I called him and we met at his home on Beattie Street in Vancouver to discuss engaging, for payment, his big band to do a concert for me as a fundraiser. We got along famously. Anyway, Dal invited me to hear his band at the Pacific National Exhibition and I must say their sound blew me out of my socks. I called Dal to start planning a concert and he told me a shocking piece of information. Dal said he could not do a concert for me because his wife worked at City Hall and it would hurt her if he did a concert for me, as Larry Campbell would likely make her pay for doing this. So, here is one of Vancouver's most respected citizens telling me that Larry Campbell could make it hard on his wife if I paid his band to perform at my fundraiser.

At this stage of things, I could not even buy a band for a fundraising event due to the Larry connection. This loss really hurt as I felt if anyone would live up to a challenge it would be a fellow musician and one of Vancouver's most respected and prominent citizens. Once again, I was surprised, very confused and quite frankly very disappointed. I felt if anyone would be there, it would have been Dal Richards. However, knowing what I know now about Larry Campbell, Dal was likely right to put his wife first.

The James Green Song
A well known teacher and former member of the group Trooper, Frank Ludwig, wrote my election song. How exciting - and it goes exactly like this:

> There's a new voice in Vancouver,
> That speaks through listening to you.
> Like a fresh breeze off the water
> A new spirit, new attitude.
> 'Cause you care about our city,
> Now your voice will be heard.
> And you want a say in how it's done.
> Now your voice will be heard.
>
> Vote James Green for Mayor.

Key Supporters

At the beginning of the campaign, when I was in my office, I had a team of advisors, a campaign steering committee and supporters. Numerous people agreed to help, such as my daughter Arlana, my wife and mentor Marlies, John Dormer former Mayor of Kamloops, family friend Tracey Gabert, long time friend Ed Miles, Steven Chong from the Tung Tsin Hakka Association of Vancouver, Frank Palmer, Dennis Law, Don Young, Leanne Gillespie, Ron Barker, my former student Myk Gordon and videographer Jonathan Moran. Also, Jim Doswell, a former Assistant Deputy Minister in the provincial government and former Liberal candidate for MP in the Richmond Delta East Riding, gave me some advice as well. I have known Jim for over 40 years. Another interesting advisor was Bob Purdy, a former City Engineer. A very supportive friend and respected television producer Kirk Shaw assisted me in any way he could; as did another TV producer, Blair Reekie. Also among my supporters were well-known TV and radio personality, Shell Busey and Maritime Museum Executive Director Jim Delgado.

CHAPTER TEN

Election Funnies
Well, it's time for a short break from the serious stuff to offer you a few humorous anecdotes.

The first joke is on Councillor Jim Green. The night before the election Jim Green was being interviewed on CBC television and he said, referring to me, that James Green is riding around on that big bus and that he, Jim Green, could not afford a bus like that. After the election, when I reviewed Vision's financial disclosures at City Hall, I learned that Jim and Vision spent $1.5mil. on their campaign. The bus cost $9000 for the 10 days I had it. With their $1.5mil. they could have afforded 20 or more big buses like mine. Instead, they went for that old fire truck with Councillor Jim Green's name on it. Why, I am not sure.

David Cadman was, and is, a city councillor. He was attempting to get re-elected and I found his record on council very interesting. I called David and left a message for him to call me. Well, Cadman emailed me and said that he had seen me at an event but I did not seem to want to talk, so he didn't approach me. Funny thing, considering it was not me he saw, as I had not attended that event. Maybe it was a doppelganger. I must say herein that David Cadman is a dedicated councillor and is working to keep the majority NPA Council honest. Hats off to you David.

Not to leave the NPA out, I recall an incident after the election when I attended a city council meeting. The meeting had not yet started when Councillor Suzanne Anton approached me with a smile, put out her hand and said nice to see you Maurice or Bob or Bill, I don't remember the exact name she used. I told her I was James Green and had run for Mayor. Red faced, Ms. Anton turned and headed to her seat without a further word to me. So Suzanne, another doppelganger, or do all black people look alike?

The funnies continue! Before the animosity, Jim Green's office had set up a meeting for me with a government official named Brian Dolson, who was an Assistant Deputy Minister Olympic Bid, Community Initiatives and Vancouver Agreement (quite the title). The meeting was at the provincial government offices in downtown Vancouver. When I rang the buzzer to gain admission, a lady came to the door and told me that deliveries were to go to the door down the hallway. So, apparently, black people comprise a large part of the courier industry in Vancouver. Another racial slip up, I'd say.

An article in The Vancouver Courier speaks for itself. Here's the essence of the Courier article.

COPE a loser with Casino
By Mike Howell-Staff writer:
> The $50,000 that Great Canadian Casino contributed to the 2005 election campaigns of Vision Vancouver and the NPA was not a payback for the parties' support of slot machines at Hastings Racecourse, says a company spokesman.

Mike goes on to say:
> In July 2004, then-Mayor Larry Campbell and Vision Councillors Raymond Louie, Tim Stevenson and Green voted in favour of slots at Hastings Racecourse. NPA councillors Peter Ladner and Sullivan also voted in favour of slots.

And then Mike drives his point home further:
> The company didn't give money to
> COPE, whose councillors at the time
> voted against the slots. Blank
> *(Howard Blank of Great Canadian)*
> didn't know why Great Canadian
> didn't contribute to COPE's
> campaign.

Nice work, Mike. You are one of the few reporters actually following the basic tenant of investigation – *Follow the Money*.

In the same article he also follows some developer money:
> Rennie *(Bob Rennie of Rennie*
> *Marketing Systems)* told the Courier
> in an October 2005 interview that he
> contributed to Sullivan's campaign to
> ensure that the other NPA Mayoral
> candidate Christy Clark wouldn't
> win the NPA nomination for Mayor.
> But he backed Green in the election
> because he believed he would make
> a better Mayor than Sullivan.

Bob Rennie is involved in the marketing and sales of condos at the $280 million Woodward's development, which was spearheaded by Jim Green. Rennie said the connection was not a reason to support Green.

How funny is this? Very! Believable? That's how business is done in Vancouver, says Jim Green.

A young reporter for the tyee.ca called me in late 2006 about the 2005 campaign. We did an interview in a coffee shop and I awaited the published article. Well, nothing came out. Two, three, four weeks went by and still nothing. I called this fellow, Bryan Zandberg, and said, "Hi this is James Green, any word on the article you interviewed me for?" Imagine my surprise when he said, "Sorry, **Jim**, we found no connection between James Green and the NPA or Sam Sullivan, so no story, yet".

He had interviewed me face to face for at least an hour and a half - for what? Now, when he thinks I'm Jim Green on the telephone, he spills the beans.

CHAPTER ELEVEN

So Where did the 4,273 votes come from?

Firstly, I spent hours at events and celebrations and dances put on by the Filipino community. I spoke at these events, shook thousands of hands, handed out flyers and cards and shared in food and refreshments. I also spent time on the dance floor at the dances.

I canvassed Chinatown with well known Chinese businessman Steven Chong, and attended several very important events there. I also visited seniors care facilities in Chinatown. I was surprised at how the seniors, and others, were briefed by their leaders to vote for the number of the candidate. I was Number 7 on the ballot and, as I was introduced, people were told to vote for Number 7 James Green. This happened all over the city and characterized the way many were briefed to vote if they did not understand the English language too well, or not at all.

A member of COPE had called me and told me many members hated Jim Green as he had left COPE with a large debt and he was a bully. Also, COPE did not run a Mayoral candidate in the election.

I canvassed all over the city, and did on-line canvasses as well. Then there are the people I knew in Vancouver for years. During my city-wide walks through the many neighbourhood centres such as Dunbar, Kerrisdale, Point Grey, the West End, East Hastings, Downtown, Downtown Eastside, Yaletown, Chinatown and Gastown, South Cambie, Marpole, etc., I met hundreds of people who committed their support. I also handed out flyers and business-style election cards to people on the street and to hundreds of businesses throughout the city. I attended a majority of the All Candidates Meetings for Mayor.

My campaign bus, with my name, James Green, prominently displayed, traveled the streets of Vancouver for no less than 100 hours. I left flyers and cards at community centres and malls. Lastly, there are the disgruntled voters who would not vote for Jim or Sam.

Relative to the hard work I did, I was surprised that I did not receive more votes than 4273. However, I lacked the funding to buy the television time, newspaper advertising, flyers and brochures, city wide door-to-door flyer drops, etc.

I also know that some of the bad press I was getting changed the minds of some voters. Relative to all other independents, my campaigning was extensive, and the votes I did receive reflected the hard work I put into my campaign.

神州時報 China Journal

October 15, 2005
Tel:604-669-2988
Fax:604-669-2999

P2 封面人物 Cover Story

"高大、英武、勵黙、親近" 的溫哥華市長候選人。他的競選口
號是"強力、廉近、改革與融合"。你也許不完全贊
同他的想法，但是不容否認他實實挺出了一些敝有
意味的新東西。

我是金詹仕

——訪溫哥華市長候選人 James Green

口張愛君 小魚

走近金詹仕(James Green)

<我與我相識>

名將人的城市的構想>

金綠社(James Green)競選辦公室

電話: 604-709-3627

電郵: jmagreen@telus.net

網站: www.jamesgreenformayor.com

Campaign Story in The China Journal Newspaper

Mayoral Candidate James Green.

by Anthony Oluwatoyin.

Hurricane Katrina just might have a local impact, after all. If the "other" Jim Green in November's race for Mayor of Vancouver, has anything to do with it.

Running as James Green, to avoid confusion with the Vision Vancouver candidate, the former Delta school teacher and trustee, believes that Katrina has already revived fears of a local big one, an earthquake, and issues of Vancouver's preparedness.

So James Green's very first piece of campaign literature mentions a review of Vancouver Security, Disaster and Evacuation, if he is elected. The notorious deadlock at City Hall, Green believes, means that Vancouverites will

Olympic Training Program High Jump Champion, says, "I can be a champion to the people in Vancouver."

That would, he says, "move Vancouver from a great city to a magnificent city" that will "set an example to the world" with the 2010 Olympics.

He has quite a plan in mind. He wants to set up Harmony Centres, a cross-cultural venture in social initiatives. He wants a Youth Advisory Board that will put issues "to the kids themselves." He wants to introduce "three strikes, you're out" to Vancouver's exploding property crime.

Mayor James Green's Vancouver would be "open for business," he says. Instead of banning Walmart, as the city just

to work with ICBC on parking incentives to promote smart car use. He wants to work with MLAs, MPs representing the area, other mayors, the Premier, on new ideas, on Drug Courts, fair sentencing, possession, decriminalization ("I don't want to turn huge parts of the population to criminals," he says) but not legalization.

A tall order, "an uphill battle," James says. He referred to "little fiefdoms" at City Hall. He believes "Vancouver is looking for a different kind of leader." Not an ideologue, he said of another candidate. "Someone who is moderate," he said of himself.

Born in 1947 at the Royal Columbian in New Westminster, his

While his rivals for the Mayor's office are busy going at each other, James Green is bubbling over with bold new directions for the city he wants to take from what he calls a "great city to a magnificent city."

worry all the more about leadership and working together in a crisis.

There's another key difference between James and Jim Green.

Jim has gone on a recent warpath against his opponents, engaging in personal attacks, causing freshly announced candidate, former Deputy Premier Christy Clark, to quip, "Jim Green ain't no Larry Campbell."

James Green, on the other hand, is content to raise the more broad-based question of the appeal of "star" candidates, like Christy Clark, a concern echoed by voters from the last federal and provincial elections.

In an exclusive with The Afro News, James was very much issue-driven, from crisis to crime, commerce, culture and community.

—The 1963 BC Junior did, he would work with the retail giant, trading tax breaks for "good corporate citizenship" and "covenants" that speak to worker issues.

He seeks similar public-private ventures, "new ways of earning revenue," with the film industry, the communications industry, with others in town.

He does not believe that this will leave the unfortunate behind. He quoted the mid-1960s, 38th Vice President of the US, Hubert Humphrey:"It was said that the moral test of government is how that government treats those who are in the dawn of life, the children; those who are in the twilight of life, the elderly; and those who are in the shadows of life, the sick, the needy and the handicapped."

He wants City Hall Vancouver roots go back to 1935, when his family started what was perhaps the city's first cabaret, The Dixie Chicken Inn, he believes it was called.

Food and music also played later roles in his life. The former ' 60s, & 70s, R&B singer, later (in the ' 90s) produced a cooking show, The Urban Peasant for the CBC.

In another era, James Green might have been treated to the backhanded compliment: " A Credit to your Race." 30-odd years ago, his brother, Truman Green, wrote a novel by that title, of interracial romance, set in 1960s Newton, Surrey, BC, nursing old stereotype with timeless longing.

Today, he says, "I don't believe being Black should be an issue." "Quite frankly," he adds,

'I have such a mixture in my family...' There is Jewish and First Nations in his heritage. The father of two (daughters) has been married for 36 years to the [illegible] Marlies.

He certainly has the range of ideas and plans for Vancouver to match such a rich background.

Campaign Article in the Afro News newspaper

Newspaper ads

Newspaper ads

and more newspaper ads

CHAPTER TWELVE

Political Philosophy
Before I go on, it is important for me to do a little philosophizing. When I told others that dirty tricks were happening to me and my campaign they said too bad, but that's politics.

I truly believe that we, as a city and a people, do not have the luxury to continue the dirty way that politics and campaigns are conducted in this city, in this province and in this country. Digging out dirty laundry, for example, just to destroy the reputation of our opponents, releasing it and not giving the target the chance to refute it, should not be acceptable. If there is something questionable about a candidate, it should be brought up at All Candidates Meetings, at debates and forums. This never happened once to me during the campaign. Sending incorrect information to the media and voters is not good enough. Make information public where the target of it has the opportunity to defend him or her self. Backroom politics, to plan an opponent's demise based on lies, must stop. Merely bringing up dirt to hurt people is not acceptable, especially if that dirt is not true. Having the dirt and muck thrown at me, somehow validated my campaign and my candidacy. Whatever it did to validate me as an opponent or candidate, it sure was some dirty stuff and hurt me with some voters.

Finally, for the media to do this is unconscionable. The media should not be a partisan election tool, but rather a news body.

Lastly, please don't believe anything written about anyone, especially during a political campaign. Do your own research. Call the target of the assault. Get both sides of the story. We must send a message that we will not accept dirty tricks, lies and corruption from our politicians and their political parties.

This piece was presented to make several points and I know you got them. Citizens should do some research and find out the truth before they commit their vote.

CHAPTER THIRTEEN

More Campaign Assaults

Once it was clear I had a serious campaign, the conspiracies, dirty tricks and lies began. What I had in place began to unravel. On the following page, read the letter Jim Green sent to all media and others around the city.

Before you read the famous imposter letter, let me give you the dictionary meaning of IMPOSTER - An Imposter, so says Websters, is one that assumes an identity or title not one's own in order to deceive. Let me be clear here, I have been called, by thousands of people for over forty years, Jim Green. My mother calls me Jim, as that is the name I went by prior to this campaign. From the day I officially began to run for Mayor, I returned to my birth name of James Green. When I filed my papers for Mayor I wrote in James Green. On all business and campaign cards it now said James. On all flyers and even on my bus it said James Green. At the numerous events I attended I was introduced as James Green. Understand, if I was running for Mayor to cause confusion and mischief, I could have kept my name as Jim Green and there would have been two Jim Greens on the ballot.

Howell, Mike (LMP)

From: citynotes@votevision.ca
Sent: Thursday, November 17, 2005 1:53 PM
To: mhowell@vancourier.com
Subject: It's JIM Green, Vision Vancouver for Mayor

It's Jim Green, Vision Vancouver for Mayor

In case you haven't heard, there's an impostor running for mayor. So on Election Day make sure you vote for the real Jim Green for Mayor.

It‚Äôs JIM Green, Vision Vancouver.

Who knows why the impostor is there. He did get an office from a big Sam Sullivan supporter and that office was in the same complex as Sam Sullivan‚Äôs suite of offices. But Sam claims he has no connection to the impostor.

No matter how it happened, it‚Äôs still a significant risk to the real Jim Green. And Vancouver. If the impostor takes enough votes through name confusion, Sam Sullivan could end up mayor.

We can't turn back the clock to the bad old days of neglect and cuts under the NPA. Do not mark your ballot for the impostor, James Green.

Look for the real JIM Green along with his party name - Vision Vancouver. That‚Äôs number 8 on the Ballot: Jim Green, Vision Vancouver.

And don‚Äôt forget the rest of the Vision Vancouver team: Heather Deal, Raymond Louie, Tim Stevenson, Heather Harrison and George Chow.

PLEASE FORWARD THIS TO EVERYONE YOU KNOW!!!!!!!!!

The infamous Imposter Letter

While writing this book, I called a few reporters to get their stories about how badly they covered my story as a candidate. The first person I called was Charlie Smith, the editor of The Georgia Straight. Charlie, in the discussion, offered the information that Vision had threatened to pull out of an All Candidates Meeting if I, James Green, was on the panel of candidates. Smith refused to exclude me and, surprisingly, Jim Green did appear.

The attempts to get me barred speak volumes for the state of mind and strategy of Vision. I am sure that Vision did this many times. But I ask you to work with me, with your logic, to get behind their thinking in wanting to exclude me from All Candidates Meetings and debates.

If Vision wanted to be sure voters knew there were two Greens and their Jim Green was the best candidate and the guy to vote for, what better way to do so than to meet me head on. Attack me with their charges of fraud and make sure the voters knew I was the other Green and that their Jim Green was the guy who voters should vote for. Also, would Vision and Jim Green not want to show voters and the media that I was the useless candidate that they were saying I was?

So, it is clear to me that Jim Green and Vision conspired to keep Jim away from me. Before I discuss the man behind the insults and dirty tricks, I wish to offer the following open letter to Larry Campbell, the former RCMP officer, coroner, Mayor and currently a Senator.

Dear Larry
You have never met me or spoken to me. You know nothing about me and my history as a teacher, community leader, father and husband. You have no proof that I have ever been in the pockets of the NPA or anyone else.

All you really know, Larry, is the fact that I was a threat to your man, Jim Green. My mere presence as a candidate was enough for you to launch a campaign of political terror against me.

I have seen your attempts to stare me down and your hateful behaviour. I surmise that you have some very deep problems accepting that I could be in any position of power in your world.

I ask you, Larry, should you not have used your skills, that you certainly mastered as a police office and coroner, to find out if the things you said about me were true or untrue? It should have been contingent upon you to research the information your people released about me, to be sure it was true before it was released.

I feel the straw that broke the Campbell's back, and your credibility, was the day you called me a criminal to Mark Marissen at Liberal headquarters. Sadly, you did not have the honesty to own up to the truth when asked about this statement by the press. I can only ask that you search deep inside your soul, Larry, and speak to your God and ask for forgiveness. Abandon your apparent philosophy that the end justifies the means.

Larry, you were wrong to defame me, slander me and suggest I have done something illegal, which I have not. I hope someday you will take the time to sit down with me and learn who I am.
Yours truly,
James Green

The Mark Marissen, Christy Clark, Larry Campbell Caper:

Like it or not, Larry Campbell is not the golden-haired boy many would like him to be or have fooled themselves into believing he is. I touched on this earlier, but here is my take on what Larry did to become a Senator. First, it is likely that the James Green Affair served as a smoke screen and focused attention away from Larry's secret.

Larry quit COPE, formed Vision Vancouver and then announced he would not run for Mayor as part of a deal he made with the Liberal's Mark Marissen. Few people receive appointments to the Senate without having something on the government, or who can be used to further the agenda of the government in the Senate. I have no proof of what Larry did for the job, but I believe Larry, Christy, Mark and the Liberal backroom boys cooked up a doozey. Larry would agree not to run. He would do so to clear the way for Christy Clark. Larry would also help cripple the NDP backed COPE, which he did by forming Vision Vancouver. So, for the promise of a senatorship, Larry would feign support of Jim Green and even help him. Deep down, Larry didn't really feel Jim could beat Christy. Jim winning was not part of the plan, so there would be no problem supporting Jim. The Liberals felt Clark would beat Jim Green, as the big money and Christy's high profile would get her elected. Larry would not be found out, as he had supported Jim Green. Once I entered the race,

Larry could use me as a smoke screen and attack me as a criminal and imposter; as a diversion away from his little lie. The architect of this scam was Mark Marissen, Christy Clark's husband. The only glitch in the Marissen plan is that Sam beat Christy because the tide in the NPA turned against Christy when the media and the public attacked her for not living in Vancouver. The NPA, once this happened, felt Christy would lose and they pushed and supported Sam for the nomination. So, once again, who won? Larry Campbell won, as his story didn't get out and he can leave as a Senator with the status of a Senator, $120,000 salary and all of the perks of the office.

Larry then worked with Mark Marissen to get Liberals, such as Hedy Fry and David Emerson, elected. Sadly, the Liberals lost the election and Larry now officiates over weddings, goes to celebrity events and sits at senate committee tables reading reports or questioning witnesses. So guess what? I am not sure who won or completed their mission successfully. Yet now I know one thing for sure. Vancouver politics and federal politics are equally as corrupt and many men and women politicians will do almost anything it takes to gain and maintain power for the sake of their party, backers and big money.

Please understand, this is a theory and I have no proof of it, but it does explain some of Larry's behaviour.

The men who planned and implemented the first conspiracy had loose morals and very low ethical standards. The chief con and master of dirty tricks was our beloved Mayor Campbell. There was another conspiracy hatched by Larry Campbell and implemented by Jim Green and Vision. It consisted of libelous statements, slander, half truths, intimidation and other bad behaviours. By now it would seem that poor Larry would do anything to get his friend Jim Green elected Mayor over Sam Sullivan. Next came Larry's minion Geoff Meggs who would do anything to hold on to his job, and the other Vision candidates who wanted to be elected. Still let's not forget Clay Suddeby and a guy named Mike McNeil.

It must be clear, none of these shameless people knew, as of August 2005, the level of backing, money and or organization I had. I had also said, in the newspaper, that I planned to spend thousands of dollars on TV commercials, radio ads and more. A year earlier I had told Allen Garr, a Courier newspaper columnist, that I planned to raise a million dollars to run for Mayor. Did they just fear my name taking votes away from Jim Green, or did they also fear I might actually be tough to beat?

I posed a real threat and had to be dealt with before I gained any momentum. With this in mind, Vision planned to ruin me before I even got out of the gate.

The fact that these unscrupulous people conspired to ruin my chances is the way politics works, some say. I do not accept this and the voters proved that they didn't either. However, their efforts motivated me to continue the fight. Their dirty tricks backfired, as Jim Green lost the election and a great deal of credibility. The fact that Vision's Jim Green lost the election is proof that the people of Vancouver rejected Jim Green's and Vision's dirty Mayoral campaign in the city. The demise of Larry Campbell's boy is a solid testament to the integrity of a majority of Vancouver voters. The fact that we got Sam Sullivan by default is just plain too bad.

NOTE: After the election it was reported that Police Chief Jamie Graham had sent a letter to the RCMP regarding Sam Sullivan's buying drugs for addicts. Larry Campbell's fingerprints are all over this plot to ruin Sam Sullivan's reputation and role as the chair of the police board. More dirty tricks, my friends. As it has turned out, Sam doesn't need help being ruined, he does a fine job by himself.

Once my picture, taken outside of my office, was in the Vancouver Sun, and the attached story told where my office was, the stuff hit the fan. I was evicted from my office. These bad guys thought I would run away with my tail between my legs. In fact, and few have heard this before, I did, for a few hours, consider packing it in. Sitting in my living room after I had been evicted, I felt beaten. However, I just picked myself up and got back in the race.

CHAPTER FOURTEEN

THE CAMPAIGN
Getting My Message Out

The part where you get your message out is based on one thing. You have to have a message before you can get your message/platform out. The media, in the four months I campaigned, treated me as if I was only a name. As Steve Burgess in Vancouver Magazine stated, I was, to the media, the Human Homonym and nothing more. In fact only two papers mentioned a small part of what I stood for and this, in itself, was slight coverage.

Matthew Burroughs of the WestEnder
Sept 8, 2005

> "Currently Green is running on a platform to "create a common ground and represent Vancouver in a dignified and respectful manner." He does not approve of the infighting that has led to the much published split within the Coalition of Progressive Electors (COPE) that helped spawn the offshoot Vision Vancouver Party. Green wants to lead the city in a way that gets beyond partisan politics."

Erin Airton of the 24hrs on Sept. 15, 2005
    "His program is pretty standard. He
    wants to build a strong economy and
    decrease residential and business
    taxes. He wants to deal with
    homelessness and drug addiction.
    And finally he wants to review
    creative solutions to the
    transportation crisis that threatens to
    cripple Vancouver. Nothing that we
    are not hearing from the NPA and
    Vision Vancouver. But there is some
    innovative stuff when you dig
    deeper: Joint ventures and public
    private partnerships and some pretty
    gutsy alternative revenue generation
    methods…"

I really appreciated these two reporters and thank
them here for attempting to be as fair as possible.
Most articles merely talked about the name game,
possible collusion and fraud. Well, for the record,
I did have a message that I attempted to get out,
but not to much avail, as the media was not
interested in finding out what I stood for, or
thought, or planned to do as Mayor. However, the
information was readily available on my flyers

and web site and I delivered it at all events and meetings I attended.

Well, the truth is I had an extensive platform. Anyone who said I had no issues did not read the thousands of flyers I handed out all over the city.

I put out a very good web site, built first by former friend Blair Reekie, and taken over by a professional company that was one of Vancouver's top web site builders.

The following speech, which I used throughout the campaign, was first delivered at SFU downtown, on Oct 17, 2005. The only candidates invited were me, Sam Sullivan of the NPA and Jim Green of Vision Vancouver.

> This election for Mayor of Vancouver is about leadership.

> This great city needs a great Mayor who speaks for all of the people and represents the interest of the citizens, not political parties, special interest groups or ideologies. The new Mayor must be dynamic, energetic and dignified and must be capable of

working with all sides be they left or right wing, COPE, or NPA or Vision. The new Mayor must have the experience of leadership and must be able to oversee council and bring an end to political infighting and bickering at the council table.

I have taught people of all ages and understand how to run a classroom, or a council, or for that matter any group. The new Mayor must be a fun Mayor and a Mayor with a sense of humour who brings passion to the position. The new Mayor must have deep roots in this city. My family's roots go back to 1935 in this city.

There are many serious issues to face and the new Mayor must be able to mould council into a cohesive, effective team that can work together to solve the problems of this city and continue to develop this great city into a magnificent city. With my over 40 years of leadership experience as a school teacher for 20 years, a school trustee for three years, an executive producer, arts administrator, athlete, musician, community board member and conductor, I have mastered the key components of leadership which are the mastery of negotiation, extreme patience and the ability to be flexible and to facilitate action. With me as your Mayor, City Hall will be more friendly, responsive and cooperative and council will be a body that bases all things on social, economic and environmental sustainability for all communities of Vancouver. Therefore I ask you to move Vancouver out of the mire of political gridlock between warring factions and elect me as your Mayor, a Mayor who you can be proud of and who is not part of the problem but part of the solution. Please vote for James Green for Mayor of Vancouver on Nov 19. Vote for a breath of fresh air and the beginning of a new era of cooperation and harmony at City Hall. With me as Mayor of Vancouver your voice will be heard. Thank you.

My Vision for Vancouver, I Repeat

My vision for Vancouver is that we become a city that celebrates its successes and that works together to correct its problems. I see Vancouver as a model city where we have strong caring leadership at the civic level that models effective problem solving techniques and teamwork for the entire world to see. I see a city that bases all things it does on economic, social and environmental sustainability. I see a city where all residents, be they First Nations, Asian-Canadian, Afro-Canadian, Indo-Canadian, or European-Canadian live together in an environment of acceptance and respect. I envision a city where law and order prevails and all citizens are expected to take responsibility and be accountable for their actions before the courts and in their everyday lives. I see a city that prepares all of its residents, rich or poor, for all possible disasters and where neighbours are committed to helping neighbours. I see a city where our seniors are treated with the utmost respect, cared for in a humane and loving manner and who have easy access to a high quality of life. I see a city that is great and that rises to its potential to become a magnificent city. This is my home, my Vancouver and I love and cherish it.

My First Campaign Manager

On top of everything I had, I knew having a campaign manager was key. My experiences with both of my campaign managers were the strangest relationships I had during the entire campaign.

She had been trying to get in touch with me for days, she said on the telephone, and finally did. Her name was Juliet Andalis and she was a Liberal candidate in the previous provincial election. She was interested in helping get me elected Mayor. She seemed to have a strong family and loved her two girls. Being married for 36 years myself, with two daughters, I was drawn to Juliet and was so pleased to have her on board, as she had been deeply involved in getting David Emerson elected and she said she could bring me thousands of votes from the Filipino community. I felt blessed having Juliet on my team.

The day after the meeting, her husband, Romeo, came to my office and brought two prominent Chinese leaders who committed to helping me get elected.

I was so excited, as Juliet looked like a fighter and she knew how to campaign. I felt I was on the way to becoming Mayor. Then tragedy struck. On Friday, September 23, 2005, I was watching the news and heard that there had been a women killed in Vancouver at 53rd and Granville. I said to my wife, that is where Juliet lives. I quickly called her and she came to the phone and cried out, "They killed my daughter". She was crying and in shock. However, she had planned for me to attend a big banquet that evening and now, even in her time of loss, she said that I still had to go to the event. I did go and had the opportunity to speak to well over 300 people that evening.

I offered my condolences to Juliet and hung up and cried for her broken heart. Some monster, it was reported, had shot her daughter through the window of her car and left her there for her family to find. Few understand the loss and the hurt a murder brings to any family. I knew all too well, as my sister had been murdered in 1970, and of course all of this came back. Juliet would be devastated for some time and I, from my past loss, could and would be a source of strength for her. My daughter and I attended the funeral and experienced the heartbreak of Juliet and her family's loss. This heightened my resolve to become Mayor and help clean up this city. Juliet did help me a great deal during the campaign, organizing appearances, handing out hundreds of my flyers and accompanying me to events. This woman had endured the loss of her daughter and still had the strength to help me with my campaign.

My Second Campaign manager

A few days after the funeral I was experiencing the loss of someone to lead my campaign. Here is the email that introduced John Fellows to me. It was initially sent to me on Friday, September 23, 2005.

> Hello Jim. My name is John Fellows.
> I would like to meet you in order to help elect you as Mayor.
> The situation with COPEless in Vancouver, the Not Paying Attention party and the blurred Vision Quest is ripe for fresh eyes and minds to represent the people of Vancouver. I can be reached at . . . . I look forward to hearing from you.

I trusted his story and his stated commitment to help make me Mayor of Vancouver.

John met me at the office. He believed that I could win and that he would do anything to help. He talked basketball, social issues and had a sense of humor. He convinced me he was the person to run my campaign. He said he was unemployed and would work full time to get me elected. He had rented a car and would drive me everywhere, which he did. He often talked about working with me in the Mayor's office. It seemed like a fit, we had a good time and worked hard together. John accompanied me to all of the All Candidates Meetings, went to City Hall with me when I filed my papers, worked on my website, and sent out emails. He also went to events at the Azure Grill and Lounge with me. He began to plan my fundraiser at Azure Grill and Lounge. John also held an executive committee meeting. We decided he would run the team and take care of the infrastructure of the campaign. I was to worry about the platform, attending meetings and publicity. All else was his to take care of. He had my password for my email and kept all contact directories. I trusted him implicitly. He even went with me to pick out my campaign bus. He knew everything. He was in charge of the steering committee, my fundraisers, and an event to be held at The Centre in Vancouver for the Performing Arts.

Once evicted from the office, we began to look for new space. I had a friend, Nizar, who had some space on Fraser Street and we went to look. After we looked, Nizar decided that I should meet Ujjal Dosanjh's main man. I met with him and it seemed to go well. However, the next day Nizar told me I had made a big mistake and that John worked for the other side. I didn't believe him. I had invested too much in John's presence and couldn't believe he was a plant, so I never told John about this conversation.

A few days after the meeting with Nizar, we went to City Hall to get a candidate's guide book. Afterwards, John told me he could not work for me anymore. John Fellows quit half way through the campaign. He took all of my information with him and told me he would take care of the website and emails that came to the web site after he left. He would pass all of these emails on to me immediately, he promised. In fact, some emails that would have helped me during the campaign were passed on to me after election day.

After writing this, I find I am still not sure. Was John Fellows a plant? Was he an opportunist who thought he saw a place for himself in City Hall? Was he threatened? Or was he just a well-meaning individual who got in over his head and couldn't go for the long haul?

Taping a one-minute campaign spot at Global Television in Burnaby. My spot was aired during the Sam Sullivan, Jim Green debate.

Asking a question of other candidates at an All-Candidates Meeting .

Taping a spot in front of City Hall for my election coverage DVD.

CHAPTER FIFTEEN

The Media

Next we will deal with the media and how they covered the story.

The best line I heard about my campaign, after the election, was written in the Thunderbird Newspaper at UBC on December 1, 2005. The author was a Richard Warnica:

> "It's amazing the difference a day can make. On November 20th, James Green was the biggest story in Vancouver. The day before, he couldn't buy a headline."

It should be asked, "Why should the media have given James Green any coverage?" Firstly, the media made the name game a major issue. This initially triggered a short-lived barrage of media coverage. Secondly, I was the only other independent candidate who has ever been elected to an office. Thirdly, no other independent candidate had the extensive web site I had, the campaign bus, or campaign office. I was the only independent candidate who had a serious campaign. Most importantly, my name was so

close to the other Green' that all questions
surrounding me should have been asked and
answered by the media. Was I a plant? Did I have
a campaign, a platform, any money, and the skill
to be Mayor? Who supported me? What was my
personal history? Could I win? Would my name
on the ballot ruin Jim Green's chances of being
Mayor? How was I planning to campaign? What
was I saying and how was I doing at events and
All Candidates Meetings? Be very clear here: I
sent requests and press releases and links to my
web site to Vaughn Palmer, Charlie Smith of the
Straight, The Bill Good Show, Fanny Keffer's
Show, Studio 4, the Rafe Mair Show, Frances
Bula of the Sun and many others. Not one of
these folks in the media would interview me to
question me about my campaign or platform or
what I stood for or what I planned to do different
if elected Mayor. They all, with the exception of
24 Hours and the WestEnder, refused to talk
about anything but the name game.

Why the media did not fully cover the story will
be dealt with as this chapter moves along. Let's
take a look at the news media and get to the
bottom of this.

No question; radio, television, magazines, newspapers and newsletters, play a very important role in our lives. News is very significant in shaping our opinions. We have 24 hour radio news programs in Vancouver. On television there are numerous news programs on every station. The news permeates our daily lives; at work, in our cars and in our living rooms. So it would seem reasonable in the context of this book to ask what the role of the news media is in political campaigns.

They tell us their role is to inform, investigate, get to the heart of the story, report the stories that are important to us and affect our daily lives. Know first, make the story clear to you, make your world an easier place to understand, is their credo. I could go on and on about the claims of the media as to what their jobs are.

Let's not fool ourselves. The Jim/James Green story was the opening excitement of the campaign. Initially, I knew it would make a few headlines, but I thought, as they got into reporting on the Mayoralty race on a daily basis, that I would pass Jim and Sam in the polls once voters knew who I was. I thought that the depth of who I was would be widely covered.

CHAPTER SIXTEEN

Welcome to the Media Awards
The Envelope Please
AND THE AWARD GOES TO

Worst Investigative Reporting Award goes to Jared Ferrie. Jared wrote for the Metro Newspaper and an online paper called The Tyee. He wrote a seemingly in-depth article on me. As you will see, Jared likely should have dropped journalism and become a romance novelist or paperback fiction writer, or something far from being a newspaper columnist. In fact, Jared can write, he just missed class the day they covered investigative reporting, research and ethics in journalism.

So what story won Jared the award?

James Barber Scorches James Green
Celeb chef no fan of former biz partner James Green
     By: Jared Ferrie
     Published: October 24, 2005
     TheTyee.ca
     James Barber has cooked up some spicy dishes since hosting the Urban

Peasant television show in 1991, but
never thought he'd be part of a recipe
for political controversy.

As the Vancouver Mayoral race
heats up, one candidate has got
Barber simmering with anger: James
Green.

After listing some background information from
my web site, Jared lets James Barber have a say.
In the article Jared quotes from my bio that I am
an expert in all aspects of the television industry
and was instrumental in the success of the Urban
Peasant. Jared writes that James Barber doesn't
remember it that way. "We bought him out," he
said. "It cost a great deal of money to get rid of
Jim Green and it was worth every penny."
*(Remember, I was known as Jim Green, as shown
by the TV program's credits which CBC used in
one of their campaign coverage spots.)*

Please remember when you read this that James
Barber is a big supporter of Jim Green and I
wouldn't be surprised if Jim asked Barber to do
this interview. Also, Jared never called me to get
my response to Barber's cooked-up comments.

Let me start from the beginning. Firstly, when I met Barber he was the Money's Mushroom Man on television. You remember "Money's Makes Meals Marvelous" don't you? He had just been fired from a proposed television series called World of Food, a program I was asked to executive produce. We met after this and decided to do a cooking series. I took the show idea to CBC and they liked the concept but doubted Barber, who had a reputation for being very difficult, could become a TV cooking show host. I convinced them to give him a try and I raised all the money, facilities and equipment for a pilot production. In fact, I put up $16,000 of my own money to finance the first pilot and negotiated with CBC to supply the cameras, crew, lighting, sound equipment and editing for the pilot. Barber ran this pilot, as he convinced me he could produce. CBC rejected it. It was a sad excuse for a pilot and Barber had failed.

I knew, after this rejection, that I would have to take over all aspects of another pilot. So I regrouped, hired a new team, raised more money, re-produced the pilot and it was accepted by CBC, not only for the original weekly of 13 episodes, but expanded to a daily of 65 episodes. I raised almost $700,000 to produce the first series of 65 episodes. I took over as the producer and executive producer. My friend, Bob Scragg, invested the cash portion of the $700,000 production budget and CBC put up the facilities and equipment for the production. In putting the cash together and taking over this project, I ironed out all of the problems with the series, including Barber's poor performance. Once the series was produced, I gained a distributor, sold between 8,000 to 10,000 books per month called the Urban Peasant. This book could not be given away before the series aired. I raised all monies for another 65 episodes once the first 65 episodes had aired. My wife Marlies and I were responsible for this show and Barber, I can say, after we rehearsed him over and over again, finally was a good host. We had the show distributed world wide.

With success, Barber became very difficult. This man of 72 often hit on woman half his age on other programs. He demanded more money than he had been contracted to receive. He constantly made mistakes on camera and included elements in the program we had not agreed to. James was constantly appearing at restaurants around the city and attempting to use his television host status to get free meals. As the executive producer I was aghast when Barber included a segment on the fact that he had fed guests cat food during the war. I called him on this, as I did not want to leave it in the show and a major war erupted on set. James, the Gem, threatened to leave the show as he marched off the set and the show was shut down for more than an hour.

Barber upset the CBC when he ended a segment with "Wham Bam Thank You Ma'am". Experts were called in to determine if this was acceptable and it was not. Barber had proven ignorance and male chauvinism were the mainstays of his character.

After more than a year as Barber's partner and executive producer, I quit the show due to his poor attitude, rudeness and troublesome behaviour. He did not fire me as Jared's article suggests. He did not buy me out because he wanted to get rid of me, as Jared's article and Barber suggest. This simply is not the truth. It was not Barber getting rid of me, it was me quitting the show and Barber having to pay me for my share of the show and buy me out as a partner.

Jared could have found all of this out by doing some research and calling CBC and me. Instead he relied on one person's side of the story. To clarify my role in Urban Peasant, on the next page I include a letter I received in 1992 from the regional Director of CBC, John Kennedy.

The three pilots Kennedy referred to were the ones Barber ran. The new pilot was produced and executive produced by me and my wife, Marlies, and directed by Lawrence McDonald. It was picked up and the series was produced. CBC had rejected the pilots Barber had run and if I had not stepped in and re-produced a new pilot, Barber would have been toast. I bring this up as Jared has not done his research and presents Barber's story as if it is the one and only truth.

To top it off Jared posted the imposter letter Jim Green had sent out about me on thetyee.ca comments pages.

Suffice to say, Jared has proven that he does not understand the importance of the truth and how to get to the truth. Once again let's hear it for Jared Ferrie. Give it up folks for the winner of the Worst Investigative Reporter Award, Jared Ferrie.

Canadian Broadcasting Corporation
Société Radio-Canada

P.O. Box 4600,
Vancouver, B.C.
V6B 4A2

August 19, 1992

Mr. Jim Green,
Executive Producer,
Urban Peasant,
c/o CBC Television,
Vancouver, B.C.

Dear Jim:

We have had a number of discussions over the past
several months about your role as Executive Producer
of URBAN PEASANT and I'd like to set a few of my
thoughts to paper.

When I arrived in B.C. I saw three URBAN PEASANT
pilots which had not attracted the interest of the
network.

After a number of meetings and discussions you
convinced me that you understood what the problems
were and that you could improve the show. I secured
the network's approval for a pilot and the rest is
history.

Included in that history are some of those
discussions to which I referred above. I would like
to repeat here what I have said to you on many
occasions; I count on your presence as the person
in charge of this show and I consider you
accountable for its successes and its problems.

I have enjoyed the working relationship I've had
with you and Marlies. That relationship is enhanced
by the effectiveness with which the two of you have
addressed our concerns about the content and
presentation of the show.

Here's to the next 65 -

Yours sincerely,

John H. Kennedy,
B.C. Regional Director

cc: Joe Novak,
    Rae Hull

                    7(a)

Letter from CBC Regional Director John Kennedy
regarding my role on the Urban Peasant cooking series.

DOPPELGANGER????

Definition: Double, twin, mirror image

I'd say it was a toss-up between the guys on the left as to who is whose doppelganger

The second award of the 2005 election goes to Bill Thielman for:

The Poorest Researched Article.
Bill's headline, Losing by a Name in 24Hrs Newspaper on November 22, 2005 illustrates why he won this award.

Here are some of Thielman's comments.
"It is obvious that outgoing councillor Jim Green would be the new Mayor today but for the mysterious appearance of a political doppelganger called James Green."

Doppelganger? Doppelganger means clone, counterpart, duplicate, twin, mate, match, double, look-alike. Jim Green of Vision Vancouver and me, James Green, are none of these. Firstly, Bill needs to learn the language or at least use a dictionary. The funniest one is look-alike. No need to comment further. Just read the entire book and form your own opinion.

Next, Thielman sites in his article that I received 4273 votes "despite running alone with an invisible campaign". Invisible means ......? Please read all of this book and tell me if Bill did not work hard to win this award. Let's hear it for Bill Thielman. No research on me, no interview, just bias, prejudice and closed eyes were behind Thielman's article. Congratulations Bill.

The Most Biased Report Award goes to Ms. Frances Bula.

Funny thing about Frances Bula, she wrote an article about the civic elections in Delta in 1987. When she wrote about my election to the Delta School Board, she referred to me as unknown Jim Green. Bula was mistaken back then as I was very well known in Delta in 1987. I had taught there for many years, run a well known arts society, presented concerts throughout the district, sat on numerous boards and I was often in the Delta media.

Remember Frances, you worked long and hard to get this award and I am sure that, for the next election, you will come in first in the slander, defamation and libel category.

So what did Frances do to win? Firstly, she was at the City Hall press conference candidate Jamie Lee Hamilton held about some charges she had against Jim Green. I was driving by City Hall and saw all of the press. I got out of John's car and walked over to see what was going on. Someone yelled, "It's James Green," and the cameras rolled. John Daly of Global News interviewed me on camera. Afterwards Bula was walking away and I asked her why she didn't do a story on me and she said I had no chance of winning and was not a credible candidate. She might do a story some day but she doubted it. She walked away from me in a rude and arrogant manner. It gets better. I guess Bula decided she owed Vision and Jim Green some help after he lost the November 19, 2005 election, or was this just sour grapes by Frances? In her article she reported about my mysterious non-existent string of bankruptcies. Let me quote from her article dated February 21, 2005 that came out two days after the election.

Head line:
Two Green's Cloud Mayor's Victory
By Frances Bula

> "....however Green's campaign appeared odd to many. He has a string of bankruptcies in his background, yet conducted a relatively energetic and well heeled campaign that included a campaign bus and an office..."

Bula is insinuating here that I was being paid by the NPA or Sam Sullivan to run, as I did not have the money to run. This slanderous innuendo in the Vancouver Sun is nothing short of actionable.

Clearly, Frances got her misinformation from the information Vision Vancouver had sent out to all media. Sadly, Frances never called me to comment or refute her misinformation before she wrote the story. I did follow up with a "string of emails" in which I tried to set her straight. I do thank the Sun for the retraction even though the story remains on their Canada.com web site (and is not linked to the retraction).

Lastly, in granting Frances Bula the Bias Award, we give you this advice, Frances. Next time, before you attempt to defame opponents to help Jim Green and Vision Vancouver, base your information on fact.

Now to the Award for Exclusion

The winner is Charlie Smith of the Georgia Straight. Charlie is a nice guy who got swept away in the media cloud of suspicion about James Green.

I emailed Charlie Smith around the time that I was making my candidacy known. The Courier had come out with a story, as had the WestEnder. When I called Charlie he seemed angry that I had not called his paper first. He asked me why I called the other papers first, when the Straight has more readership than WE and the Courier. After this conversation our joust by email began.

----- Original Message -----
From: Charlie Smith
To: jmagreen@telus.net
Sent: Friday, September 23, 2005 6:15 AM
Subject: Georgia Straight response
    Hi James,
    Thanks for the fax and the e-mail
    information. I am still planning our
    municipal election coverage.
    You've gotten lots of coverage in the
    local papers. I am still trying to
    come up with an original angle so I

don't just look like I'm repeating everyone else.

We'll have more coverage as we approach the election. I must confess that when I first learned about your candidacy, I wondered if someone who doesn't like the other Jim Green had paid you to run. After I confirmed that you were a Delta school trustee, I realized that you are a serious candidate.

Charlie

And finally, after much back and forth dialogue in which I laid out some of my platform and reasons why he should give me some coverage, Charlie wrote the following reply.

-----Original Message -----
From: Charlie Smith
To: Jim Green
Sent: Tuesday, September 27, 2005 8:21 AM
Subject: RE:

You're winning this argument, James.

I may have won the argument, but I did not win any ink in his paper. So Charlie gets the Media

Exclusion Award. Surprisingly Charlie was a victim of conventional thinking, and conventional thinking, coupled with lazy thinking, is usually wrong.

My scrap with Charlie Smith from the Georgia Straight is representative of the media's overall attitude that they have the right to determine who the public should vote for, or even see, during an election campaign. They also think that they have the right to say who has the right to run and what qualifications a candidate should have. These boys and girls also, once they have made up their minds, will give those they pick to be the front runners unlimited coverage while they ignore any other contenders, even if covering a contender would best serve the public.

Before I get on with the awards I wish to print a letter my wife Marlies wrote, but did not send to the media as she was sure all would have cried bias because she is married to me, a candidate.

Shame
How is it that, in a democracy where a basic right is that of running for office, the media can prejudicially discriminate against candidates who all meet the qualifications to run for office -

equally? Especially during this, 2005, the Year of the Veteran, how can we honour those who fought for our freedom, yet so blatantly squander those very freedoms - shame on you.

There are 20 candidates running for Mayor of Vancouver, all of whom have met the requirements. As of the day they are officially accepted, they are all equal. If the requirement system is flawed, it must be addressed. Meanwhile, step up and honour the process. Present all the candidates. Who is to say who should be presented, invited to speak, debate and be heard. Allow the voters to make an informed decision. Present all the candidates, not just the ones who can crawl deepest into the richest pockets.

Does this artificial culling by the media really allow the best candidate to be chosen - democratically? Of course not - Shame on You. While we proudly wear our poppies, we must also proudly wear our democracy and allow the process to play out fully.

And for those who say "That's politics," double shame on you for your complacency.

CHAPTER SEVENTEEN

Let's take a brief interlude before presenting the biggest media award of the election. Here are some honourable mentions for coverage, both good and bad.

The Province

During the campaign the Province did some huge coverage of Jim Green and Sam Sullivan, but gave me a few lines and no photo. Though this was far more than any other Independent was receiving, it represented that the media did not know what to do with me and gave big coverage to those who bought big ads in their papers. I also sent numerous press releases to all papers and not one was printed or mentioned in the media, including the Province. So for all intents and purposes the Province ignored me and I could not get their attention.

Rafe Mair Show

Regarding radio, I was called by Rafe Mair's producer and was invited to guest on his show for 15 minutes. I felt this was great, but because of his last minute interview with Stephen Harper, my interview was cut to five minutes and he only asked me about the name game, why I was running and could I win. It was far too short and it was ironic that Rafe was fired the next day.

CKNW

I spent much time calling the Bill Good Show and emailing them. The producer, I forget her name, told me they would be getting back to me during the campaign and I would have a chance to be on the show. I was never called, but did hear Jim and Sam on the Bill Good Show several times. I was ignored like all other independents.

24Hrs

This paper did give me the best story as their writer, Erin Airton, actually mentioned I had a platform. She mentioned some of my ideas and gave me some credibility as a viable candidate. 24hrs deserves accolades here for at least recognizing my platform though my brand of no partisan politics was referred to as sweet and naïve. What still confuses me is there was no picture.

Metro

Jared Ferrie (winner of my Worst Investigative Reporting Award) of Metro did an article after he had interviewed me, but the article did not mention my platform and ideas in depth.

Shaw

Shaw aired a debate and profiles of the
candidates. This cable station made best efforts
to bring the candidates and their platforms to the
public and they should be congratulated.

The Vancouver Courier

Though the Courier seldom wrote about who I
really am and what my platform was, they
certainly gave me more coverage than the other
papers. Reporter Mike Howell also sent me the
information Vision was circulating. Howell did
follow up on all stories and called me for my
input before publishing a story. This is called
good investigative reporting. When I release my
platform next election we shall see how well the
Courier and Howell cover it.

The only problem with the Courier is a reporter
named Allen Garr. Garr, like Bill Thielman of
24hrs, may as well be a minion of Vision
Vancouver as he cannot see the other side of any
question.

I contacted Allen in August 2005, and he
promised to get back to me after his holidays. He,
of course, did not. To this day Garr has stated or

intimated that I just appeared at the last minute to run for Mayor. Remember, I told him I was running for Mayor when I met him at City Hall in 2004.

The Globe and Mail

This paper surprised me as I had some respect for it. However, a reporter named Gary Mason from the Globe called me a day or so before the election for an interview and merely talked about Jim Green vs. James Green and did I think I could win. I would have thought the Globe would have followed the story earlier and put some depth behind their report. No such luck.

CBC

A CBC reporter called me and told me they wished to cover me, my candidacy, what I stood for, etc. and arranged an interview with me. I was, of course, very happy to get this coverage before the election. Well, the reporter and a camera lady came out and set up what they were going to do for the next half hour. The reporter interviewed me on the bus, taped me getting off of the bus, meeting and greeting people on Cambie Street and speaking to business people. The story, she assured me, would be a profile of me and my campaign and what I stood for. I asked her, at the end of the interview, when the piece of approximately 5 minutes would play and she said on Canada Now at 6 pm on CBC. I was very pleased and went home.

At 5:55 pm that day I got a call from the lady who had done the interview. She apologized for the fact that the news director had edited the story and it was nothing that she had promised it would be. Again, this surprised us. We turned on the television, and what we saw shocked us. The piece had been edited, and left out the interview and anything about me, who I am, or what I stood for. Instead, it merely showed me a few times and focused on the name game and the question of did I work for the NPA. It showed Jim Green expressing his worries and concerns that I could cost him precious votes.

Overall the story was nothing that the reporter told me it would be. So, in a state of surprise, I called the news director. He added fuel to the fire when he responded to my complaint with, who did I think I was getting a big bus and expecting coverage. He said he had the right to edit the story and tell the story any way he liked; basically, too bad and I had no right or basis to be upset. I said that I should not have been told what the story would be if it was not going to be this. He said that they did the best they could and I should not be complaining about the story.

I wasted 40 minutes of my precious campaigning time for a story that had little to do with what I was promised and more to do with the name game and Jim Green's worry about losing votes to me.

Business in Vancouver
This paper had no shame in the way they covered the campaign. They put out two editions. One had a large picture of Jim Green on the cover and an interview and the other had a large picture of Sam Sullivan on the cover. Both had a headline that read "The Men Who Would be Mayor." Now this disturbed me as the article referred to Jim and Sam as the only candidates for Mayor as if there were no others, when in fact there were 20 candidates in total.

BCTV Global
Again, I was called and invited to appear on a debate with the Mayoral candidates, Sam and Jim. I was pleased, but once again what they sold was not what they had told me.

I received another call to tell me there were too many candidates so they would allow only Jim and Sam the debate time. The other 18 would be taped for a one minute segment to be played on the air on Global during the same news hour that Sam and Jim's debate would be broadcast. I called the news director Ian Hayson and he said he would re-consider my being on the debate with Sam and Jim. I never heard from this guy again and the one minute spots were all independents would get.

At least they gave all the Mayoral candidates some time, and my one minute spot was introduced on camera and appeared during the middle of Sam and Jim's debate.

FLASH: I called Ian Hayson, the news director of BCTV Global Television in early February 2007 and asked him if Jim Green or his boys had called him to threaten that Jim would not appear on the Global debate if I was included. Hayson told me that he remembered something like that, but would have to speak to the producer of the debate and he would get back to me. As of February 10, 2007 I had not heard from him. However, Hayson finally had a lady from his office call me who told me, in true Watergate fashion, that Mr. Hayson has no knowledge of Jim Green or Vision calling to block me. My assumption is that Jim Green had made the threat and that is why I was uninvited from one of the biggest media events of the campaign.

CHAPTER EIGHTEEN

Now for the biggest and most important media award.

The Media Platinum Buffoon Award

The winner of the Media Platinum Buffoon Award is CTV News reporter, Ron Brown. Rob worked hard to get the story wrong. He reported false information about Sam Sullivan getting me my office and illustrated that he lacks ethics, fairness, journalistic integrity and good common sense. Rob's parents and colleagues should be proud of him. To show Rob's genius, let's present his award winning story here.

Let me set the stage. It was being said everywhere that Sam Sullivan helped me get my office in the Plaza of Nations. People like Larry Campbell said, on camera with Rob, that if he (me, James) was being supported by the NPA, then it's reprehensible and I don't know what actions could be taken. Jim Green said this is exactly what they expected all along and it's a sad situation that it has come to this. Rob Brown said he asked Jim what can be done about it and Jim indicated to him there was very little he could do, but he did say he would be getting in touch with his lawyer. All other newspapers and radio and television reporters based their reports on Rob Brown's story that Sam had helped me get my office.

The following has been copied from Rob Brown's report, on CTV, following the election.

Rob Brown: Well, we tracked down Julius Simon, the owner of the Azure Restaurant who calls Sam Sullivan a friend and he tells a very different story. He insists that someone from the NPA camp did indeed help James Green. That someone was Sam Sullivan himself.

Rob Brown: Who asked you to give James Green the office?

Julius Simon: Sam, he asked, you know, if I can help him, you know, for with this office.

Rob Brown: Let me just be clear. You're saying Sam Sullivan asked you to provide the office space for James Green.

Julius Simon: That's right, yeah. He said you know can you help you know James you know with the office. I said no, I can't because I don't have any space.

Rob Brown: Sam said that?

Julius Simon: Yes.

Rob Brown: Now again to be clear. What Julius Simon is saying is that Sam Sullivan came to him at one point during this campaign and asked him to provide office space here in the Plaza of Nations for James Green, free-*(pause)*-of-*(pause)*-charge. Now that, in spite of the fact that Sam Sullivan has always maintained, did so including this afternoon, that he had no connection at all to the James Green Campaign.

As well as speaking English poorly, Simon understands English even less well. In short, a very poor witness to the alleged crime, Rob; and you must have known this. Also, why not interview Simon in person and not on the telephone?

Now let's look at this closely and scientifically. Julius said he told Sam he had no space. Brown ignores this comment. Remember the headline here is that Sam Sullivan made a call to Simon to provide me with a campaign office in the Plaza of Nations free of charge. We have to ask, how could Sam have gotten me the space when Julius was clear that he had no space. Sam actually called after I was evicted to see what had happened, why I was evicted or to see if he could get me the space back; and maybe to raise a little dirt on Jim Green. During the interview Simon never mentions money. Rob has it wrong and the above interview proves this. Although *"at one point during this campaign"* is a nice bit of journalistic doublespeak. It lets Rob squirm past the fact that everything he is talking about is after I was evicted from my office. I initially got my office on my own, before Sam was the NPA Candidate for Mayor.

Moreover how does one call, that had no positive results for me, constitute Sam being involved in my campaign? This one call is the only example of anything Sam did, and in fact I did not get the office back so no help at all. Granted, he probably should not have made any call, but how does this represent what Jim Green, Larry Campbell and Vision Vancouver charged; that Sam Sullivan helped James Green with his campaign? It does not. Rob take heart. You have won a prestigious award.

CHAPTER NINETEEN

All Candidates Meetings and Events
These meetings were very important to my campaign for Mayor. They were generally set up very well. I compliment all organizations who sponsored an All Candidates Meeting as they are true believers in the democratic process. I felt I did very well at these meetings and they were a great deal of fun, as well as being informative. Yet Jim Green seldom stayed for the entire time and usually left early, especially if he was receiving a rough time and difficult questions.

I was invited to The Vancouver East Cultural Centre Arts debate on October 14, 2005.

Dear James Green
On behalf of the arts community of Vancouver, and its many patrons, I am writing to see whether you would be available to participate in a moderated debate on the Arts and the role they play in the future of the City of Vancouver on Sunday 13th November at the Vancouver East Cultural Centre.

We will have a series of questions
from both the public and arts
practitioners. – We foresee questions
which include arts and the Olympics,
arts and education, arts and
community, arts and investment, arts
and capital expenditure and much
more.
Councillor Green and Councillor
Sullivan have both accepted this
invitation. The CBC and Georgia
Straight are covering this event.
I look forward to hearing from you
at your earliest convenience.
Duncan Low
Executive Director
Vancouver East Cultural Centre

The debate was to be moderated by a fellow from
CBC Radio. I was sure I would make a good
impression as I had the most outstanding
background in the arts. I had been a music teacher
for 20 years, an arts administrator, a ballet
company manager, founder of arts non profit
groups, a professional sax player, singer and
marketer of concerts across the country. As a
Delta School Trustee I was known as an arts
advocate assuring that our district had an arts

coordinator and trained arts teachers in our schools in Delta. I had been an arts department head, president of the Delta Arts Council, and choir teacher. Compare this to Jim Green's limited arts background as a member of the Board of Directors of the Vancouver Opera Association, and the man who brought performances to council meetings. Sam had been in a band and perhaps some other arts experiences I do not know about. So, here we had a meeting to discuss the arts and I felt I was the most qualified to do so.

Then the most surprising thing happened. I arrived home one afternoon and there was a message from Duncan Low of the Vancouver East Cultural Center. He was uninviting me from the Arts debate. I was outraged and called Duncan and told him so. He said he could not do a thing, because, when he invited me, he did not know how many candidates there were and CBC wanted only two, Sam and Jim. This logic, as to why I was uninvited, to this day makes no sense, but does represent what Vancouver politics can be like. It is supposition here but I believe that Jim Green merely said "get rid of James Green or I will not be there". Whatever, I was not to be part of this debate. I did sit in the audience and remember how the whole event went into shock as Darryl Zimmerman, a not-invited candidate for Mayor, insisted on having his time. He sat down at the candidates table as if he had been invited. He wailed on his sax and was asked to leave. The organizers were very upset with this and I somehow felt this was Karma for Duncan and his organization. I did call Duncan Low after the campaign to see if he could tell me why I was uninvited. He has never returned my call.

FLASH: It's January 2007. I just checked the Vision Vancouver website and found a picture of Duncan Low. He is a director of Vision Vancouver. Okay, so did his cancellation of my invitation to the Arts event have anything to do with his alliance with Jim Green and Vision Vancouver?

And I will pose the question again. If you were Jim Green would you not want James Green present at every All Candidates Meeting to show who's who and how much better you were than James? Wouldn't you want to challenge him head on in public?

As well as these events, I attended meetings at the West End Community Centre where I made a stir and spoke of Jim Green's poor negotiations of the Woodward's Project and my vision of Vancouver. I attended meetings at the Carnegie Centre in the Downtown Eastside, The Roundhouse put on by the Gay and Lesbian Business Association, Heritage Hall, False Creek Elementary, Van Dusen Gardens sponsored by the Real Estate Board of Greater Vancouver, two events at UBC, a drop-in sponsored by a theatre group and a youth forum at a pub in Gastown.

CHAPTER TWENTY

Policies and Press Releases
These following policy statements and releases are examples of what I stated I would do if elected Mayor in 2005. As this book is being written, I am developing new, innovative platform planks for release in 2008.

NOTE. I sent my website and address to all media, sent them press releases, and my flyers and cards included my website address. There should be no doubt that the media could have discovered my platform, policies and priorities, if they desired.

Unfortunately, none of these documents were printed and my platform and priorities never saw the light of day in the media. The dueling Greens story was big. My platform and what I stood for was lost. So let me take this opportunity to introduce you to some of these documents.

Press Release
October 19, 2005 For Immediate Release
Mayoral candidate James Green stated today he is fed up with the city's fruitless and passive lip service to supplying social housing in Vancouver.

"We need 1000s of units and we need the funding to build them. The community raises millions for other causes and crises and we must mobilize to raise money for social housing. The city must refocus its priorities." He went on, "The city, senior levels of government, the private sector and all citizens must get on board."

"We are losing money on Woodward's, covering a \$13.5 million shortfall and granting the developer a \$6.5 million interest free loan. I say take a closer look and scale Woodward's back. Put money into social housing outside of the Woodward's Project". He asked, "Who negotiated this bad business deal in the first place . . . and we are also selling city land to the developer? Wrong again", said Green. "Lease it to them and put the lease money into social housing. The Woodward's and False Creek Flats Projects may break the bank. The city leaders at council better put the brakes on and redirect their efforts to the plight of those who do not have decent housing in this city. Let me be clear," he went on, "I do not discount the importance of the development community and the good work many are doing. I am not anti-developer or development. I am just pro-social housing," he said. "My approach is not against anything."

"The lack of social housing is a disgrace and a crisis and it must be addressed now and aggressively. We must move on it now, not after the political parties debate it, and commissions and planners study it and others review it to death. The locations must be selected, the plans completed, the process cleared, the money committed and all other preparations completed. Construction must get going before this crisis gets any more out of hand. We, in fact, should include the development community in this as they have the expertise."

"We have the world coming here in 2010 and we will be a disgrace if we do not address our social housing, poverty, crime and homelessness problems NOW," he said. "Are we not learning anything from New Orleans?" he went on. "Do we need a major crisis to show us the poor living conditions some face in this great city of ours? People need help with food, clothing and shelter, and a step up in this city. The longer we put it off the more dissention, unrest and pain we allow to grow. In turn, the problems negatively affect all of us. All people of the city must be mobilized to solve the social housing crisis and as Mayor I will lead this endeavour and get the housing built. "

"There is no question about it," said Green, "It will take leadership and commitment and the will to succeed. I grew up without indoor plumbing and with tarpaper siding and I know what it is like to not have good housing. It is not a happy experience," James Green went on. "The city has dropped the ball and it's time for the leaders of this city to pick it up and run with it. Lastly," Green said, "it is not a left, right, NPA vs. COPE vs. Vision football to kick around for political gain and votes. It's a social issue we must all address together - Now."

Press Release
No Tax Increases, New Revenue Generation and New City Auditor General, Highlight James Green's Economic Program
James Green, who is running for Mayor of Vancouver as an independent candidate, says he will not support further tax increases during his tenure as Mayor. "I will do everything I can do to stop increases beyond inflation," stated Green.

"A new corporate culture must be established at City Hall where the Mayor and council work as a board of directors who keep the financial interest of the taxpayers, first and foremost in their minds" said James Green.

"To improve the overall fiscal management of the city I will form an independent committee to appoint an independent City Auditor General whose exclusive job will be to audit the city's finances to see if we are getting value for our money. The Auditor will report quarterly and highlight problems before they turn into monsters," said Green. "No one including the Mayor and council will be immune", said Green.

"Also," said Green, "We will spend what we can afford to spend, even if we have to downsize or scrap some projects, and be more efficient. We must commit to giving our citizens a breather and allow them to have more money in their jeans." said Green. "We will hold the line and do only what we can afford", said Green. "I am committed to generating new revenue and profit centres through public private partnerships, joint ventures, and investments," said Green. "We must gain increased funding from senior governments as part of our strategy." said Green. "This will take innovation," he said. "Through a Mayor's Economic Advisory Council comprised of the top labour, business and financial people in the city, we will develop a corporate strategy to manage the city's fiscal house on strict business principles rather than political will", James Green stated. "We will also look at inviting big business here and gain their commitment to participate in the city's social and other costly programs", said Green.

In closing Green said that, if elected Mayor, he would bring an entirely new approach to city finance and fiscal management to the table.

CHAPTER TWENTY-ONE

The Big Black Bus Appears

"James, are you gong to stand on the various bridges like Burrard, Cambie, etc. with signs? You also need a couple of big vans or buses with your picture driving around all day."

This email from Frank Palmer gave me the best idea of my campaign, gave Jim Green and Vision some ammunition, got me tons of the attention I needed and was partly responsible for the number of votes I received. The bus served as a boardroom, office and a spectacle nobody could forget. What a great boost it was and I thank Frank Palmer for the email.

So I received the idea of a lifetime and looked over bus companies in the phone book. Charter Bus Lines was my choice and I called to set up a meeting. After looking at all the buses they had to offer, I went for the Exec. as it would get the most attention.

I left Charter Bus Lines of BC, and when I got home I started calling supporters. One said he would help me with the money, $9000. At the final hour the money did not come, so I called the owner. He said he would work with me and he did. The bus arrived at my house on November 9, 2005. The bus got me back in the game and I planned to take full advantage of this moving sign, office and excellent mode of transportation.

The bus, now known as The James Green Bus, was a stroke of genius on one side and a target for my detractors on the other. Imagine, the dirty work had been done; I am defamed in the media, the office is closed, the campaign manager has resigned, the money is not there to the amounts I needed and I get this machine with my name on it. "40 feet of black magic" I called it. The only problem was that my picture was not on the bus as I had ordered.

As the President of Charter Bus Lines described it in the Vancouver Sun on November 26 under the Headline "James Green Under Scrutiny over Executive Campaign Coach."

> "Sometimes used by the prime minister when he is in town, it's an unbelievable bus like a traveling boardroom," says Sheldon Eggen, the president of CBL , which rented the bus to James Green, originally

for 19 days. "There's only one in Vancouver like it. It's kind of like a limousine but it's way more comfortable than a limousine."

After losing my office, this machine became my campaign headquarters. This is a full view of the bus that caused such a kafuffle. It had a boardroom, shower, washroom, kitchenette, area seating with tables and came complete with driver.

Canvassing

As you may know, meeting people is the best way to get the pulse of the voters and your fellow residents. Where did I, with my invisible campaign as Bill Thielman called it, go to meet people? Well here goes. Here is my path for 10 days of the campaign From November 9 to November 19, 2005.

We traveled throughout Vancouver on the Big Black Machine. I walked along all of the major streets of the city.

I walked Dunbar Street from Southwest Marine Drive to King Edward on two occasions while the bus traveled up and down these streets. I handed out flyers and introduced myself to all businesses on the route and to hundreds of people on the street. My script was, "Hello, my name is James Green and I running for Mayor of Vancouver. Could I give you my flyer?" Some common responses were, "Oh you're the other Green, good luck". "I didn't know there was another Green, you have my vote." "Oh you're the James Green everyone's talking about, good to meet you." One guy who I approached just truthfully said "F off I'm voting for Jim Green". Many asked my position on a good number of topics.

I did not have enough money or time to canvass houses to the level I would have liked, and I did not have the money to buy newspaper, television and radio ads. However, my canvassing schedule was extremely broad. I traveled to Kerrisdale, Marpole, Hastings. I walked from the PNE to Main Street. I canvassed in the West End on Denman Street perhaps four times, Main Street, Chinatown, Downtown on Robson and Hornby, in front of The Carnegie Centre on Hastings four times, Commercial Drive three times, Fraser Street, Broadway, Point Grey and I visited a majority of Vancouver's neighbourhoods, community and cultural centres.

Juliet Andalis and her people dropped my flyers at homes. I covered businesses, movie sets, restaurants, and stopped people on the street. The bus was on the road for 10 days for 10 hours per day. When I was not on the bus, it was traveling all over the city. Remember the bus had my name on it in big letters and thousands of people saw me and I introduced myself as James Green. "No Visible Campaign, Green came from nowhere, Green is a mystery."

With my daughter Arlana meeting people outside of our campaign bus.

Handing out flyers and attracting attention while mainstreeting in Yaletown.

Volunteers Tracey and Carol being briefed before we leave the campaign bus to hand out flyers.

Email campaign
On top of all of this, my daughter also sent out hundreds of emails announcing my candidacy and requesting that recipients view my web site and respond with their questions. Many people did.

Be clear here. I reached thousands of people directly through canvassing.

The Filipino Community
Even though her daughter had been murdered, Juliet still wanted to help me win. This wonderful Filipino Canadian women introduced me to the leaders of the Filipino community and I was invited to up to ten events where there were attendees ranging from 200 to 500. I spoke at all events, handed out my flyer, shook hands, danced and hundreds confirmed they would vote for me. The commitment in this community means a great deal as the leaders, if they endorse you, have the influence to deliver 1000s of votes. Listen in to my introduction at a dance at the old Main Street RCMP hall by a leader named Romeo Mercado. Mr. Mercado is a strong leader and well respected in this community.

"Ladies and Gentleman, he is former School Trustee, school teacher,

executive   producer   and
businessman. He wants to give
Vancouver   citizens   more
opportunity,   responsibility   and
accountability. Please welcome the
next Mayor of Vancouver, James
Green." I received this kind of intro
even if other candidates were
present. Juliet also has many friends
in the Chinese community and took
me to several seniors facilities and I
was invited to a very large event on
Chinese Independence Day as well.

Juliet, and the leaders, confirmed that I would get
thousands of votes in this community, but
something happened the week of the election as
the 4273 votes I did get did not reflect their
promise. I do not want to be like Vision here, but
my intuition tells me some untrue information
about me had gotten through, or someone had
bad-mouthed me. Whatever happened, I must say
that these people are the hardest working, most
fun loving and positive people I have met. I hope
I can help them gain the recognition, attention
and notice they deserve as a major force to the
betterment of Vancouver.

ames Green with new Philippine Consul General Minerva Jean Falcon

During the campaign I was very proud to meet the new Philippine Consul General, Minerva Jean Falcon.

Making a campaign speech at a community event.

With my first Campaign Manager, Juliet Andalis.

Dancing up a storm at an event during the campaign.

Enjoying a laugh at an event during my campaign.

Smiling and happy to be included in a photo during one of
the events I was invited to attend.

In serious discussion about campaign issues.

Being introduced at another event.

Vote James Green
for Mayor of Vancouver on November 19, 2005

- Born In the Lower Mainland, Vancouver resident.
- Strong and effective leader, communicator and consensus builder.
- Elected to Delta School Board-former School Trustee.
- Former Public School Educator, 20 years experience
- Former arts administrator and arts and entertainment marketing consultant.
- Businessman, and television executive producer/financier.
- Independent of political interests.
- Married 36 years, 2 adult daughters.
- Graduate Simon Fraser University Professional Development Program.

Strong, Independent, Innovative, Effective Leader

Mayor James Green's Three Year Preliminary Platform:

- Complete review of fiscal priorities and expenditures.
- Review of major projects such as RAV Cut and Cover, Woodward's, and South East False Creek Project.
- Decrease crime, drug use, poverty, homelessness, and hunger through full funding and implementation of the Four Pillars Program and the H.O.P.E. (Health, Opportunity, Prevention and Education) Program.
- Increase community policing and community safety Initiatives.
- Vancouver Security, Disaster and Evacuation Review.
- Property tax reform and increased revenues through New Revenue Generation Initiatives and Profit Centres.
- Social housing and people with disabilities housing projects.
- Evaluation and refocus of city's densification and development plan.
- Redefine roles of city management and councilors and a meetings Code of Conduct.
- Arts and sports and business Coalition.
- Tourism and City Joint Venture Projects such as a passport to Vancouver Project.
- Multicultural acceptance Centres and more ethic group representation at city hall and in public safety agencies.
- Community, labour and business Economic Advisory Council.
- GVRD Mayor's Council for fair sentencing and effective detention.
- Youth Advisory Council and new Youth Activities. ie Indoor water surf parks, indoor track and Mayor's Youth Fitness Program.
- Community participation through a Citizen's Assembly.
- Small Business Enhancement Program.
- Transit Riders Incentive Program.
- Increased Funding for Women, Seniors, Children and Youth Support Services.
- Yearly Vancouver City Celebration.
- Animal Rights and Public Protection Program.

Please email me your list of questions or your top three priorities you want your mayor to focus on. Email your questions or concerns to jmagreen@telus.net or call (604) 709-3627

I handed out thousands of these flyers throughout the city during the campaign.

JAMES GREEN
for
Mayor of Vancouver
Strong, Innovative, Independent Leader

On Nov.19 Vote: **Green, James** | **X**

For Information - 604.709.3627   jamesgreen@telus.net
www.jamesgreenformayor.com

This business card was handed out throughout the city.
It was also stapled to the flyer.

This is the mock-up of my campaign bus signage. To my
chagrin, when the bus arrived the picture was missing.

CHAPTER TWENTY-TWO

The Name Game
The right to stand for office is not negated because of a person's name. Have no doubt, I did everything I could, within my budget, to be sure there was no doubt or confusion about who I was and that I was not Jim Green. I called the Elections Office and asked if I could change my name for the ballot. Remember, throughout the Lower Mainland I was known as Jim Green for 57 plus years. My mother, wife, daughters, friends, casual acquaintances, business associates, the phone book knew me as Jim Green.

Maybe the guy who said I probably lost votes to Jim Green had a stronger point than he even thought he did.

Students, their parents, teachers, audiences, broadcasters, all knew me as Jim Green. Legally I could have run as Jim Green. But I changed back to my birth name, James Green. Once I had done this I thought, and I still do, that Jim Green and James Green were easy to differentiate. To help this along I called all media and told them I was running for Mayor. Furthermore, I met with Jim Green and told him I was running. I canvassed all over the city as James Green. I printed and distributed thousands of flyers with my name and picture on them. I handed out business cards with my picture, name, web site and contact information. I had my name - James Green - placed on my bus that traveled to all areas of the city. I stood on street corners and introduced myself as James Green to scores of people. I went to seniors homes as James Green and attended ten All Candidates Meetings as James Green and I spoke at numerous events as James Green. The city put up a website where Jim Green and James Green were listed amongst all 20 candidates for Mayor. In fact, the city circulated a booklet of candidates and that book showed pictures and profiles of Jim Green, Vision Vancouver and James Green for all to see.

The Afro News, An Indo Canadian Newspaper, a Filipino newspaper and the China Journal all carried headline pages with my picture, name or platform and advertisements.

I have included a copy of the card I handed out, which clearly shows my face and my name, both backwards and forwards. Trying to use Jim Green's name? I don't think so.

GREEN, James

Vancouver is a great city and by working together we can become a magnificent city and a model to the world. As an independent mayor I will be answerable to one group-you the people of Vancouver.

There are many issues to resolve but the new mayor and council. However, I believe the key issue is leadership. I have been in leadership positions for over 40 years. I offer you my commitment to excellence in leadership and most importantly my team building skills. As the mayor of Vancouver I will listen and act on your voices. I will make every effort to base all decisions on social, economic and environmental sustainability. My commitment is to offer all citizens more opportunity, more responsibility and greater accountability.

My family roots in Vancouver go back to 1936. I have a great respect for this city and its citizens.

Contact
Phone: 604-709-9827
Email: jimegreen@telus.net
Website: www.jamesgreen4mayor.com

GREEN, Jim
Vision Vancouver

If I'm elected mayor I plan to build on the work I started with Larry Campbell: make Vancouver a city where citizens feel safe; where nobody is left out; where transit is rapid and business thrives.

I want to move Vancouver forward, not back. And I'll have a plan with real solutions: A plan to increase safety, to make Vancouver easier to get around, to help small business and ordinary homeowners and renters.

I'm passionate about this city. I know how to listen and the importance of

compromise, but I can make the tough decisions. It's hard work to make things happen and I'm up to that challenge

That's my commitment to voters. I'm not in politics to warm a seat. I'm here to help build a city our kids will be proud of. On November 19th, I ask for your support for Jim Green and the Vision Vancouver team.

Contact
Phone: 604-340-2140
Fax: 604-630-9003
E-mail: support@visionvancouver.ca
Website: www.visionvancouver.ca

HANSEN, Mike

Photo not available

I will swear on "Oath of Allegiance" and not an "Oath of Office." I will redirect City Halls' attention to the Downtown East Side Homelessness and drug issues. Harm Reduction is the key to the 4th pillar of the Four Pillars approach. I will implement a working 4th pillar.

Contact
Phone: 604-329-9729
E-mail: dideliot9@gmail.com

HASKELL, Peter Raymond

Photo not available

I am very unhappy with the $220 million Woodward's project. It will have nothing to do with helping the homeless since the 200 low-cost housing units will be for people on the social housing wait list, a list that not one homeless person is on. You would save money buying each of those 200 people two houses, one to live in, the other to earn rental income with.

I am for 96 Southwest Marine Drive being made not into a Walmart but a progressive homeless shelter. During my campaign I will sell anti-homelessness pre-bonds that will go

towards the homeless obtaining free monthly bus passes.

Contact
Phone: 604-321-2126
E-mail: Haskell_10@hotmail.com

HATTEM, Joe
(Maple Ridge)

My campaign focuses on enforcing the idea of democracy by giving citizens more power to decide what happens in their communities and city by hosting weekly discussions where issues and topics of concern may be addressed and prioritized. I want the best for the city I was born in so I've strategized a list of upgrades necessary for that to happen. Our city needs a real leader with the courage to hear the voice of the people and dedication to finish what is started.

With me as mayor:
- Western Canada we will be ready for major disasters.
- Trouble areas in the city will be restored to beautiful scenery.
- Vancouver will be a safe and fun city for future and existing generations to grow old in.

If you want a serious mayor with ambition, creativity, commonsense and devotion to Vancouver and it's citizens then Vote for Joe on November 19th.

PEACE!

Contact
Phone: 604-618-4615 (msg)
E-mail: easthavenjoe@hotmail.com
Website: www.604lockentlines.com

This brochure, sent out by the city, was available in all city libraries and community centres.

Candidate List

City of residence is Vancouver unless otherwise shown (in brackets and italics).

Mayor
1 to be elected

SUDAY, Zoltan

CRANGEY, Great E.

CROSSMAN, Arthur
(Coquitlam)

D'AGOSTINO, Frank M.

ESTI, Eliot

GRAY, John Landry

GREEN, James

GREEN, Jim
Vision Vancouver

HANSEN, Mike

HASKELL,
Peter Raymond

HATOON, Ine
Maple Ridge

MACLEOD, Malcolm S.

MORA, Pedro
(Burnaby)

POWER, Ray
(Burnaby)

SIMPSON, Ian W.

SPENCER, Austin
Vancouver's Internet Party

SULLIVAN, Sam
NPA

WEST, Ben
Work Less Party

YEE, Scott

ZIMMERMAN, Darrell

Councillor
10 to be elected

ANBOS, John W.

ANTON, Suzanne
NPA

APPLEGATH,
David Wilson

ARLIN, Greg

BALL, Elizabeth
NPA

BALLANTYNE, Beverley

BASS, Fred
COPE

BOYER, Marc

BRIERE, Don
(New Westminster)

BRITTEN, Patrick
Nuda Green Party

CADMAN, David
COPE

CAPRI, Kim
NPA

CHANG,
Michelle Jasmine

CHOW, George
Vision Vancouver

DEAL, Heather
Vision Vancouver

DURBON, John Patrick

HAMILTON, Jamie Lee

HARDWICK NYSTEDT,
Colleen
NPA

HARRISON, Heather
Vision Vancouver

JENKINSON, Valerie
NPA

JOHNSON, Lee

LADNER, Peter
NPA

LEE, B.C.
NPA

LEUNG, Ronald
NPA (Burnaby)

LIVINGSTON, Anne
Green Party of Vancouver

LOKE, Phyllis
(Richmond)

LOUIE, Raymond P.
Vision Vancouver

LOUIS, Tim
COPE

MALIHA, Patrick
NPA

POTVIN, Kevin

ROBERTS, Anne
COPE

STEVENSON, Tim
Vision Vancouver

THOMPSON, Kashi
NPA

WANGLEEBEN, Steve

WENDTTHIRTEEN

WOODSWORTH, Ellen
COPE

This second brochure was sent to all homes in Vancouver and clearly shows the names, ballot order, political parties and residence if not in Vancouver.

This information, part of the brochure that was sent to every home, clearly shows that voters can receive assistance if they were confused.

If you have any questions, or require additional information, please contact:

City of Vancouver Election Office
450 West Broadway
Vancouver, BC V5Y 1H3
Phone: 604.873.7681 Fax: 604.873.7734
vancouver.ca/vote
voter.questions@vancouver.ca
TDD/TYY Service for the hearing or speech impaired:
604.873.7100

English is my second language

If you or someone you know cannot understand the ballot or instructions given in English, please ask for help. Most voting places have election officials who speak languages other than English and who may be able to assist you.

You may also bring someone with you to act as an interpreter. That person must make a solemn declaration that he or she is able to make the translation and will do so to the best of his or her ability.

Sample Ballot
▼

BRITISH COLUMBIA

nber 19, 2005

BALLOT MAY DIFFER

t the OVAL

oice(s) like this ⬤

16 Yes	Candidates for
LLOR	PARK COMMISSIONER
than (10) Ten	Vote for no more than (7) Seven
First Name	☐ LAST NAME, First Name
First Name	☐ LAST NAME, First Name
First Name	☐ LAST NAME, First Name
First Name	☐ LAST NAME, First Name
First Name	☐ LAST NAME, First Name
First Name	☐ LAST NAME, First Name
First Name	☐ LAST NAME, First Name
First Name	☐ LAST NAME, First Name
First Name	☐ LAST NAME, First Name
First Name	☐ LAST NAME, First Name
First Name	☐ LAST NAME, First Name

Other opportunities to vote

If you are a patient in an acute care hospital or live in a long-term or special residential care facility, you may be able to vote where you are located. To find out more, ask at your care facility or call the Election Office at 604.873.7681.

If you are unable to go to a voting place because you have a physical disability, illness or injury, you may vote by mail. If you want to vote by mail, you must first get an application form by calling the Election Office at 604.873.7681. Then a mail ballot package will be sent to you by mail after November 2, or you may have someone pick up a mail ballot package from the Election Office for you.

Mail ballots must be returned to the Election Office before 8 pm on November 19, 2005 to be counted.

Voting procedures

At the voting place, before you are given a ballot, you will be asked to sign a declaration that you are entitled to vote, that you have not voted before in this election, and that your current residential address is correct.

The City of Vancouver uses an automated voting system that counts votes quickly and accurately. On the City of Vancouver ballot, you will see a red oval similar to this (⬭) to the left of the name of each candidate or question. Fill in the oval to the left of your choice with the special pen provided like this ⬤.

You must not vote for more candidates than are to be elected. Doing so will spoil your ballot. You may, however, make fewer choices if you wish.

If you mark your ballot incorrectly, or otherwise spoil the ballot, you may return your ballot to the person in charge and obtain a new ballot.

After you have finished marking both sides of your ballot, bring it to the automated voting machine and the ballot box attendant will feed it into the machine for you. The machine then reads the marks you have made and stores the information electronically on the machine's memory card.

For more details on the voting process, go to vancouver.ca/vote

CITY OF VANCOUVER, BRITISH COLUMBIA

Saturday, November 19, 2005

DEMO BALLOT. FINAL BALLOT MAY DIFFER

To vote, fill in the OVAL
to the left of your choice(s) like this ●

Candidates for **MAYOR** Vote for no more than (1) One	Candidates for **COUNCILLOR** Vote for no more than (10) Ten	Candidates for **PARK COMMISSIONER** Vote for no more than (7) Seven
LAST NAME, First Name	LAST NAME, First Name	LAST NAME, First Name
LAST NAME, First Name	LAST NAME, First Name	LAST NAME, First Name
LAST NAME, First Name	LAST NAME, First Name	LAST NAME, First Name
LAST NAME, First Name	LAST NAME, First Name	LAST NAME, First Name
LAST NAME, First Name	LAST NAME, First Name	LAST NAME, First Name
LAST NAME, First Name	LAST NAME, First Name	LAST NAME, First Name
LAST NAME, First Name	LAST NAME, First Name	LAST NAME, First Name
LAST NAME, First Name	LAST NAME, First Name	LAST NAME, First Name
LAST NAME, First Name	LAST NAME, First Name	LAST NAME, First Name
	LAST NAME, First Name	LAST NAME, First Name
	LAST NAME, First Name	LAST NAME, First Name
Candidates for **SCHOOL TRUSTEE** Vote for no more than (9) Nine	LAST NAME, First Name	LAST NAME, First Name
	LAST NAME, First Name	LAST NAME, First Name
	LAST NAME, First Name	LAST NAME, First Name

Sample ballot in the same brochure that went to every home in Vancouver.

CHAPTER TWENTY-THREE

The Call for an Inquiry

Two days after the election, Vision Vancouver and Jim Green called for an inquiry into what they called the James Green Affair. This was based on the CTV story and the false information that Sam Sullivan and the NPA had helped me get my office, the fact that I had a campaign bus and a web site. The Vision people called a press conference and announced they were calling for an inquiry as what they said they suspected had now been proven. When this happened I sat at home and knew the truth would prevail.

It is disconcerting to watch others accuse you of wrong doing, knowing full well that their charges are false and based on their inability to take responsibility. Jim Green, Vision Vancouver and Larry Campbell needed a scapegoat and I was it. Larry needed a smoke screen to cover up his secret, and I certainly supplied it.

Just imagine my surprise, after all of the dirty tricks and stories Jim Green had told, Jim's rude behaviour, Larry's comments in Whistler, Larry convincing the Police Chief to call for an investigation of Sam in the middle of an election, the imposter letter and the attempted and successful exclusions; now this crew was calling for an inquiry. How sad, but I invited anything that would show, once and for all, that I had done nothing wrong, legally or ethically. Apparently, the Attorney General, and anyone else they may have called for help, including the police, knew they had no case or evidence. To lay a charge, or for the Attorney General to call for an inquiry, there would have to be proof. Nothing came of this. Next, I knew these little devils were lying in wait for my financial disclosures as they hoped there would be something to fuel the charges that Sam and the NPA, or their friends, financed my campaign. Well, I am sorry, but there is nothing untoward in who contributed to my campaign. Go to the city website and see my financial disclosure. No big cheques, no help from anyone, except a few friends and a few businesses. Perhaps we should review Vision Vancouver's disclosure reports, as well as the NPA's, to see who supported them.

BIG FLASH!!!!!!
The Vancouver Sun reported January 17, 2007 that a Vision Vancouver contributor, a John Lefebvre, was arrested by FBI agents at his home in Malibu. He was charged with conspiring to

promote illegal gambling by transferring billions of dollars of cyberspace bets placed by US citizens with offshore gaming companies.

The relevance to this book is that this gentleman, in his offering to investors, stated that transferring the proceeds of Internet gaming, was illegal and therefore represented an investment risk. The most relevant part of this story is that John Lefebvre donated $170,000 to Jim Green's and Vision Vancouver's campaign. Did Jim Green not read the offering or investigate who this guy was? Who benefited from the $170,000? Did Jim Green, Larry, and the Vision Vancouver candidates not investigate this guy before they accepted the $170,000 or were they so desperate that they would accept money from anyone? This should clarify my point that these people, Larry Campbell, Jim Green, Geoff Meggs, Clay Suddaby, McNeil, and others in the Vision gang, are highly questionable in the area of trust and judgment. However, I will give the benefit of the doubt to John Lefebvre, as he is innocent until proven guilty. The story and the trial will allow us all to pass judgment once the verdict is in. Did Jim Green accept proceeds of crime knowingly, or not? Time will tell.

No one should be surprised at what poor sports will do once they have lost a competition. The excuses, the blaming, the charges, insults, innuendoes, slander, libel, defamation, and hate added up to one thing - Jim Green and his gang could not admit to themselves that they lost when they had been so sure of a victory. However, the facts were the facts. Jim Green lost the election on his own and I did not play a role in his demise. He had lost two other elections and I was not running against him in those elections. He managed to lose them on his own. So why blame me now?

CHAPTER TWENTY-FOUR

I Understand

In retrospect, I now understand the behaviour of Jim Green, Larry Campbell, Vision Vancouver, Sam Sullivan and the NPA during and after the campaign. All of these people had been, and still are, entrenched in adversarial, partisan party politics at the civic level. None of them had ever taken an independent seriously and saw me as a nuisance and a threat. The majority of independents, over time, had never launched a serious campaign like mine.

They were conditioned to learned behaviours and traditions and were not prepared to deal with or accept a candidate who did not fit their perception of what a Mayoral candidate should be. Certainly, they felt an independent like me had no place in their game. Due to their stereotype of independents, they were not open to anyone who broke this mold and who came uninvited to their game.

Like all who form biases and who fear the unknown, it was not surprising they rejected me, trivialized my campaign and refused to allow me to play as a full-fledged member of their club.

Due to all of this, their only focus was the name game. This gave them a means to deflect or reject me, the interloper, and stop me from playing the game that they had played for decades by their rules.

Having said this, I hope you will understand what really happened with my campaign, who I am, what I stand for and all of the whys, who's, how's, what's, when's and whereases associated with my campaign to become Mayor of Vancouver. I hope my entry into the race, my campaign and this book will set the stage for independents in the future and open the minds of the media and others to the fact that different does not necessarily equal bad.

This has been one of the best, most educational and rewarding experiences of my entire life. I now understand how important it is to have the participatory democracy we enjoy. The thousands of people I met, made speeches to, joked with, shared ideas with and greeted on the streets of this city made the election an illuminating experience.

The communications I received, both good and bad, are a testament that someone is out there and someone cares about elections. Here are a few of the good emails.

October 06, 2005
Dear Mr. Green
I don't usually vote, and don't have to look any further. I really like your style and have a good feeling about you. We need something different in this city.

November 8, 2005
Subject: Blast from the past
Mr. Green
James is an experienced executive producer...hosting his own local program Stage of the Arts.
I appeared on that show back in 1988. That Stage of the Arts" tape was shown at my 40th birthday party in April this year. Anyway I have moved back from LA and live in Vancouver now and you have my support.
Anyway, best of luck

Monday November 14, 2005 11:28 PM
Subject: James Green for Mayor
Hello James

>We're pretty impressed with your biography and will be voting for you on the 19th. We did research on the internet, as thoroughly as we were able, and by far you seem to be the most eligible and impressive candidate by far!

>Our best wishes to you and Good Luck on the day.

November 14, 2005
Subject: the election
Dear Mr. Green

>I have looked at your web site and see that there is a rally downtown on Thursday evening. Will you be speaking or will there be any other occasion when we could hear you speak? Even on the radio perhaps?

>We are none too happy with the other Mayoral candidates and find your approach refreshing and intelligent. It is unfortunate that you are not getting more press time.

>Thank you for letting us know

November 19, 2005
Dear Mr. Green
    We are going off to the polling
    station-and I just convinced my wife
    to join me in voting for change at
    City Hall

November 21, 2005
    I just saw on line that Jim Green is
    saying that there was some kind of
    conspiracy to do with the vote. If
    some kind of investigation or inquiry
    comes of this you can use my name
    as one that voted FOR YOU, NOT
    jim green. You may contact me in
    this matter if you wish.

November 21, 2005
    I think it was a great showing to
    come in, for the first time, with a
    bronze placing. Great learning
    experience for all. Now the work
    begins for 2008

November 23, 2006
> Gotta tell you Mr. Green, I respected
> your straight talk on CTV News.
> Good on ya man

November 18, 2005
Thank you Mr. Green
> I most appreciate your personal
> responses. I will be sharing my high
> opinion of you with some fellow
> Vancouverites, friends, professionals
> and co workers.
> You have a solid vote from me and I
> hope others will follow.
> Thanks again

This sampling tells me I did some things very
well. They are just a few of the many
correspondences, verbal and written, that showed
support. However, I did some things wrong as
well. So now let's see what we all did right and
wrong in the 2005 election for Mayor of
Vancouver.

CHAPTER TWENTY-FIVE

The NPA
The NPA did one thing right - THEY MARKETED SAM SULLIVAN very well. They did this as well as COPE marketed Larry Campbell when he won the Mayor's job.

Readers, just read this book and go to council meetings and you will find out for yourselves if Sam as Mayor is any better than having Larry Campbell as Mayor. Yes, they marketed Sam well but the NPA team sold Sam Sullivan as something he is far removed from. The photos of Sam on billboards and flyers showed a vibrant leader who would work for the good of the city. He is not.

Sam was marketed as some sort of folk hero, capable of beating anyone who dared to challenge him. He beat Christy Clark and this win created the illusion that Sam could accomplish anything and as Mayor he would be able to make this city a better place for all. Sam's spin doctors placed Sam in a position that he could not possibly fulfill. This is not to attack Sam, however the truth should prevail.

Sam has bought into the spin of his greatness and has promised things he cannot possibly achieve. Face it, Sam Sullivan does not have the skill or personal power to be Mayor. I realized this during the election, and thought voters would see through his thin veneer. No such luck.

I can only comment on this from a post-election perspective. Sam can't end the infighting and dysfunction at City Hall. He committed to this during the campaign. I have attended numerous council meetings and Sam was, and is, in the process of reversing many things the last council did, just to be vengeful. This is making council dysfunctional. So the mistake Sam and the NPA made was to make promises they could not keep or never intended to keep. For me this may be politically great. For the city, Sam has become a major liability. For the sake of all, let's hope Sam catches on and ends this very bad approach. If he does not, it will not be hard to beat him in the next election, as voters wanted action and Sam is not delivering. In fact, all of the NPA Councillors are making a big mistake. They are voting party line, instead of what is good for the city. During the election Sam and his gang told us they would successfully deal with crime, business and business property taxes, development, poverty,

homelessness and being sure the Olympics are
financially well-managed. For their own good
they should have written implementation action
strategies to be successful. Lastly, the big mistake
the NPA made is backing Sam in the first place.
Sam cannot chair a meeting properly and does not
supply the strong leadership this city cries for. If
they had to go with Sam, someone in the NPA
should have at least helped Sam prepare to be
Mayor. Instead, Sam has become a spin doctor
himself and dictates policies and procedures,
fully expecting the other NPA Councillors to vote
party line.

Vision Vancouver
Vision went wrong because they ran a negative,
mean spirited, deceitful, dishonest campaign.
They based their Mayoral hopes on a man who
had lost two elections and who was an NDP hack.
They dressed up a devil in sheep's clothing and
thought they could sell this to the voters. They
did not anticipate the negative reaction from
voters to Jim Green's unsavory demeanor,
condescending approach to other candidates and
obvious belief that he would be and deserved to
be Mayor. Entitlement never works. They
underestimated Sam Sullivan and his team of
strategists and spin doctors. They forgot that

voters don't necessary accept spin. They tried to sell Jim Green as a man of the people, while most know him as a bully. Vision missed this and it hurt them greatly. Politicians must tell voters exactly who they are and what they stand for. Vision missed this point and tried to clean Jim up and make him appear statesmanlike.

In the context of this book, it is clear Vision did not know how to deal with me. They merely ignored me in public, while behind the scenes tried to destroy me. They did not attack my policies and did not engage me in any form of debate. If Vision, Jim Green and the rest of the gang would have fought a fair and open campaign they may have captured the election. In the end they were the victims of their dishonesty, distortions, half truths, personal attacks and mudslinging. Beyond this, Vision Vancouver should have stayed within COPE and never formed this so called middle-of-the-road party where Jim Green and Larry Campbell rule and appoint candidates.

Vision Vancouver should never have run Jim Green for Mayor in the first place. If they had a more marketable candidate they may be the majority on council now with a Vision Vancouver Mayor.

Let's let Councillor David Cadman have the last word on what Jim Green and Vision Vancouver did wrong and why Jim Green lost the election.

Headline The Tyee
COPE Lone Councillor Sheds No Tears for Green
Cadman says chance to reunite was nixed.
By Sam Cooper
Check theyee.ca for the full article

> As David Cadman sees it, Jim Green paid the ultimate price for leaving COPE behind. While much has been made of independent candidate James Green possibly stealing votes from Jim Green and handing the Vancouver Mayor's chair to Sam Sullivan, Cadman says it's not true.

He goes on to say Jim Green should take responsibility for his actions and for the division from COPE instead of using me as an excuse. He felt Jim Green's attitude of entitlement was his undoing.

Cadman also said that the unions desperately wanted a unified left slate, but Green's organization turned a deaf ear when union reps came forward with reunification suggestions at an opportune time, when Larry Campbell was appointed to the senate.

By this time, Christy was out, Sam was in, Jim Green figured he could beat Sam and Senator Larry had kept his commitments. No need to change anything.

James Green
Firstly, I was right to follow my calling to get involved in politics again and to follow my passion to become the Mayor of Vancouver.

Secondly, I followed my dream and belief system that nothing is impossible.

Thirdly, I initially did most things right. I had a team, a huge advertising company on my side, a sound plan to raise money, a campaign office and a respected and able campaign manager. I made inroads and gained support in many communities.

I was flexible and came up with the Bus; an innovative response to losing my office. Overall, I truly believe that I was the best candidate. Being independent was a strength Sam and Jim could not offer. Please remember, the Mayors of Surrey and Richmond are independent, so it's not so strange after all.

I did not listen to John Dormer and I did not take his warnings about Vision Vancouver, Jim Green and Larry Campbell seriously. I did not set up my campaign to deflect the mud they would sling at me. I thought I would have to show what I stood for and the fact that I would be a better leader than Jim and Sam, and the voters would elect me. I trusted that the voters would judge these guys on their records and I would be elected. In short, I allowed myself to be out-gunned and out-monied by the NPA's and Vision's spin doctors and fundraising machines. I did not anticipate their ability to control the media. I didn't accept the fact that Larry Campbell and his plumbers had such power and could reach into so many areas of this city.

CHAPTER TWENTY-SIX

What is Ruining Politics?

What is ruining politics is that everything is spin. It does not seem that the truth can compete with the spin that the spin doctors and candidates can put on a story, true or not. This is what is wrong with the media as well. It is not the actual story the media necessarily focuses on, but how they can spin a story to make it more attractive to their viewers, listeners and readers.

This trend in spinning began with the phrase "it needs to appear to be".

During the election, Jim Green, Sam Sullivan and their respective teams spent more time putting what they thought was a good spin on me rather than getting to the meat of my story. After the election, Vision Vancouver and the media spun one telephone call Sam Sullivan made into a vast conspiracy; and spun this into proof that Sam and the NPA helped me and paid me to run. One phone call, and a dumb one at that, was spun into a smoking gun. They all spun this one call to the Manager of the Azure restaurant as proof that a plot existed. They had no proof of anything untoward. Vision and the media out-spun themselves. Jim Green's spin became less believable than Sam's and this lost Jim the election. Sam's team put a spin on Sam as a conquering hero and now Sam is the Mayor and is in far over his head. They created a Sam that really didn't exist. My weakness, it could be spun, is that I didn't spin a response to their spin. And I really didn't understand the dirty spin they would attempt to put on the James and Jim story and the spin that I was not a credible candidate. Along with their spin, and to make it more believable, Vision added untruths to their spin. So I say to the spin doctors, spin on your spin. To Jimmy and Larry, accept that you spun out of control. Sadly due to your spinning, Jim Green will never be Mayor, so spin away. All this spinning is making me nauseous.

Some Reforms
All candidates should have to gather no less than 500 signatures before they can run. The fee to registrar as a candidate should be at least $500 to $1000, not just $100. Furthermore, contributions should be limited to $5000 from individuals and $1000 from companies. Currently, there is no limit to the amount of money a party or candidate can accept. A donation, like the $170,000 that Jim Green and Vision Vancouver accepted from

an individual, should not be allowed. Furthermore, all contributions should be reported before election night. Let's make this entire thing transparent.

I think voters need to expect better of their politicians, of the media and of all people involved in campaigns. Candidates must run an open, honest and transparent campaign. They must gain the media attention, establish a large and strong political army and get the message out. Most important, they must stay true to their beliefs.

After running for Mayor and attending council meetings, I am fully convinced that party politics at the civic level doesn't work.

At the council level we need to take action and get things completed. We need to set targets and schedules for completion for all things. We must rid ourselves of partisan party politics at the civic level. The party system has caused constant hold ups, political battles and non-action at the council table as the NPA, COPE and now Vision posture and oppose each other's ideas based entirely on partisan politics. As Mayor I will have to deal with this but I will be able, as an Independent, to do what is good for the city while working with all councillors regardless of what party they belong to. At this time and place I would like to put forward a prototype of my dream councillor. I am not sure any of the current councillors make the grade, but if some of the current people are re-elected, I will work with them to become members of the James Green Dream Team. One other thing, I implore all voters to vote for the person not the party in the 2008 election and to look for these traits in a councillor.

1. Once elected, can put away partisan politics and act as an equal, non-confrontational and non-combative member of council.

2. Have a firm grasp of new and innovative ideas to solve the city's fiscal problems.

3. Action and innovation oriented.

4. Willing to champion causes in the community.

5. Able to vote their conscience and what is good for the people of the city.

6. Energetic and driven, while being balanced in all things they do as councillors.

7. Can understand and articulate the problems facing the city.

8. Decisive and engaging public speaker.

9. Have compassion, empathy and care for those less fortunate in this city.

10. Committed to strong fiscal and social reforms.

11. Committed to the democratic process.

It could be a valuable exercise to see if any of the current councillors possess these traits.

CHAPTER TWENTY-SEVEN

The Last Word

I now clearly understand that politics Vancouver style can be dirty. If I am elected Mayor, I will work to improve this situation. This experience, when coupled with all of the challenges I have had throughout my life, made me stronger than I could ever hope to be. The excitement of meeting people all over the city, dealing with the media, attending All Candidates Meetings, developing a platform, trying to raise money, hearing from old friends and acquaintances; the whole thing was fulfilling. Learning who the people of this city are, what they expect of their leaders and what their priorities are has been a learning experience I will take into the next election.

I will be running for Mayor in 2008, God willing. I invite the media to give me, and all candidates, fair coverage. I beg voters to do their jobs and do the research necessary to know who all of the candidates are and what they stand for.

New people must get involved in civic government. Young people must get involved. All races and cultures must be involved in campaigns as supporters and candidates. Women must become more involved as well. The lip service politicians give to getting the young involved and the talk of appreciating the many races and cultures of this city is just that, talk with no action. It truly saddens me that the current council, at the time of the writing of this book, has been in office for more than a year and little has been done to tackle the serious problems of the city, beyond political debates, buck passing, expensive studies, and infighting.

However, I still feel public office and public service is the greatest calling one can embark on and invite all of you to get excited about how your city is governed. There is hope, as the letter below from a young man I met in the Downtown Eastside during the 2005 campaign, illustrates.

To James Green
November 2005
Hello there.
> I'm the 'A-Political' kid you met on the street today. I don't believe I introduced myself at the time, so my name is Brodie Muskett. What you said to me earlier really got me thinking. Initially I spent the latter half of my walk thinking of a reply

that would justify my skyward nose
at participating in political events,
but then I realized that you were
absolutely right. Now's the time for
my generation to get off their asses
and do something to change the
situation! It now seems so teenaged
of me to say I'm not voting,
especially considering what could
happen in the next ten years if the
wrong people are chosen to make
decisions...

Anyway, I just wanted to let you
know that you've inspired me to get
registered and toss in my two cents. I
believe now that my generation has
the power to become aware and
make better choices for the future of
not just the municipality, but the
country as a whole.

Also I'd like to say that your
platform envelopes everything that
should be enveloped. It seems very
honest and logical compared to a lot
of what I see on the horizon today.
In fact, the fact that you were talking

to me, in that neighborhood, says a lot about who you are.

Anyways, Good Luck!

Brodie Muskett

Influencing this young man to get involved is so positive and heart warming and gives me hope that there can be positive change. Vancouver has the possibility of solving its problems if we all act collectively and in a peaceful, non-combative, non-partisan manner. A new era based on electing individuals who will serve the best interests of all citizens, will allow us to break away from our tradition of confrontation and battles at the council table.

This is a wonderful city for most of us. As long as we do not forget those that are less fortunate, we can thrive. I look forward to working with all individuals and groups and consider the possibility of becoming the Mayor of Vancouver one of life's greatest opportunities.

James Green

James Green lives in Vancouver with his wife Marlies. James is currently a marketing and business consultant and television executive producer. He is active in his community and can often be found at Vancouver Council meetings. James' passions are his family, music, writing and politics. James hopes to be elected Mayor of Vancouver in 2008.

James invites all readers to comment on this book by emailing him at jamescarlgreen@shaw.ca

Printed in the United States
By Bookmasters